Managing Externally-Funded Projects

By

Parviz F. Rad
PhD, PE, CCE, PMP

Copyright © 2007 by Project Management Excellence, LLC.

All rights reserved. No portion of this book may be reproduced, stored in a retrieval system, or transmitted in any form or by any means—electronic, mechanical, photocopying, recording, scanning, including the right of reproduction in whole or in part in any form, except for brief quotations in critical reviews or articles, without the prior written permission of the publisher. For information, contact the publisher.

The information in this book is distributed without warranty. Although every precaution has been taken in the preparation of this book, neither the author nor the publisher shall have any liability with respect to any loss or damage caused in any manner by the information contained in this book.

Published by Project Management Excellence, LLC,
5 Dell Lane, Berkeley Heights, NJ, 07922

Rad, Parviz F.
Managing Externally-Funded Projects
ISBN 978-0-9798195-0-6

Printed in the United States of America

Dedication

I Dedicate This Book

To My Grandson

Benjamin Cyrus Rad

Acknowledgement

The author wishes to thank Dr. Vittal Anantatmula for reading the manuscript and providing many helpful suggestions.

Table of Contents

1.	Introduction	1
	1.1. Nomenclature	11
2.	Proposal Phase	17
	2.1. Proposal steps	23
	2.2. Goals of the Proposed Project	34
	2.3. Estimating The Real Cost Of The Project	43
	2.4. The Bid Or The Price Of The Contract	47
3.	Contract Phase	53
4.	Performance And Monitoring Phase	67
	4.1. Earned Value	78
	4.2. Client Relations	82
	4.3. Organizational Attitude Toward Projects	85
	4.4. Management Structure	87
	4.5. Project Management Professionals	93
	4.6. Project Management Career Track	97
	4.7. Staffing Considerations	101
5.	Contract Modification Phase	107
	5.1. Accelerated Delivery Issues	112
6.	Delivery Phase	121
	References	127

Preface

Outsourcing has become a practice of choice for many industries, thanks to an increase in standardization of the processes in many specialized disciplines, and thanks to the advancements in managing virtual projects. Thus, many organizations might find themselves to have become either the client organization or the performing organization of an externally-funded project. Normally, outsourcing is accomplished through broadcasting a request for proposal, and prioritizing the responding proposals from the prospective performing organizations.

A performing organization will prioritize the proposal prospects through a model in order to develop a manageable list of projects for which to develop proposals; the model is founded on profits, staff capability, and organizational aspirations. In turn, once the proposals are received at the client organization, the proposals will be ranked through a prioritization process which is intended to highlight the most qualified performing organization; this model is founded on the organizational strategies of the client organization, and the prospective contractor's likelihood of success in the forthcoming project.

Once the contract is awarded, the mission of the manager of this project is to maintain the original real-cost estimate of the project as the internal baseline; and the contract price as the external baseline. If and when the real cost of the project to the performing organization becomes higher than what was anticipated during the proposal stage, the project manager will request an increase in the internal budget of the project. Since an increase in the internal budget will minimize the performing organization's profit, the project manager will have the additional delicate task of requesting the client organization to increase the contract price. Whether, and the extent to which, the client organization chooses to increase the contract price will depend on the project performance attributes and whether the incremental costs were incurred as a result of the actions of the client organization.

This book deals with the topics of proposal development, and contract performance, from the perspective of the performing organization. Chapter one of this book highlights the distinction between internally-funded projects and externally funded projects, and highlights the issues that are specific to the latter environment. Chapter two deals with the efforts that are involved in preparing a successful proposal, usually through a formalized proposal development process. Chapter three deals with the intricacies of drafting a contract for a prospective project. Chapter four deals with the efforts involved in successfully executing, and gracefully monitoring, a project towards completion, in line with the contract. Attributes of a sophisticated, and project-friendly, environments are discussed, highlighting how project success can be fostered. Chapter five covers the issues involved in changing the price of the contract in the light of changed circumstances of the project. Chapter six deals with the contract delivery and project closeout. The issues involved in using project data for improving internal efficiency, and in setting the groundwork for securing follow-on projects from the same client, are addressed.

Parviz F. Rad

1. Introduction

Contracts and projects are very closely linked to each other. Sometimes projects need contracts for their completion, and sometimes projects are created as a result of contracts. At one end of the spectrum, there are cases where the manager of a large project, a complex program, or a major operation, chooses to outsource a portion of the work to another organization. In this case, the success of the larger project will partly depend on the success of the contract that created the smaller project. Therefore, the manager of the larger project, which is now the client of the smaller project, will assure that the larger project specifications dictate the binding

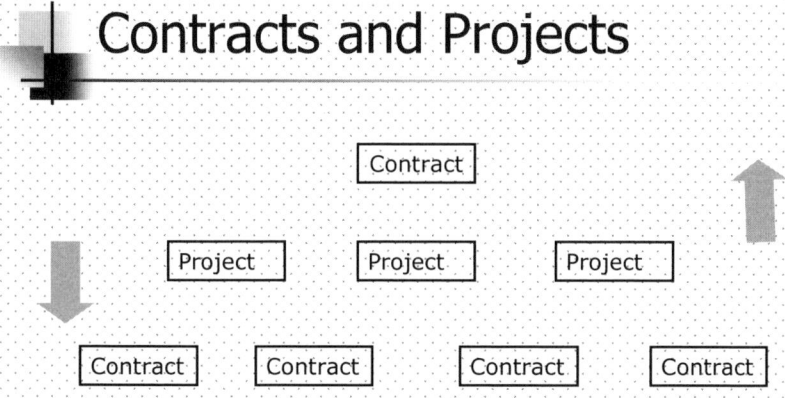

Figure 1

clauses of the contract, which in turn will govern the deliverable specifications of the smaller project.

At the other end of the spectrum, there are organizations that do most of their business as contractors or subcontractors to external clients, and most of their projects are the direct result of contract awards. Therefore, the livelihood of these organizations depends on successfully executing projects for external clients through contracts. Since the specifications for the deliverable of an externally-funded project are controlled by the contract clauses, it stands to reason that, in externally-funded projects, contract elements assume a central importance, relative to the project components. (Figure 1- 1)

This book focuses on issues of relevance to performing organizations, and the contract-related organizational functions that make management of externally-funded projects different from management of internally-funded projects. Formalization of project management activities, and adoption of a project-friendly culture, are addressed as the means of achieving success in project management, independent of the sources of project execution funds, but particularly in a performing organization environment.

In order to accelerate the accomplishment of certain urgent missions, sometimes organizations choose to acquire resources from outside the organization through a contract for the purposes of the missions of a project. This process is aptly called outsourcing or contracting, interchangeably. The decision to outsource is primarily dependent on the strategic objectives of the organization, in that it signifies that the organization is intent on achieving a certain objective which is beyond the capacity or capability of its current workforce. Alternately, it is possible that the organization collectively has the right competencies, but the distributed infrastructure characteristics of the organization would preclude an expeditious execution of the project. The decision could further be based on the anticipated competencies of the prospective external team, in that the intended performing organization might have been presented as possessing exceptional skills in a specific area. Other factors contributing to an outsourcing decision include market conditions and competitive aspirations of the organization, and the hopes for a quick achievement of certain goals through outsourcing. Some organizations opt for outsourced projects with the intention of getting immediate access to specialized skills and equipment, and with the hopes of gaining expertise in that specific area through exposure and observation. Since the hopeful expectation of skill osmosis does not always materialize, outsourcing tends to become a self-perpetuating process; for better or for worse.

Another contributor to the increase in the number of externally-funded projects is that organizations in many industries tend to diversify, globalize, and expand their operations; and the most expeditious and most cost-effective approach appears to be outsourcing. Therefore, the practice of outsourcing projects is likely to grow thanks to increases in international competition and market globalization. Other drivers of the transition toward outsourcing include a noticeable increase in global standardization of the processes in many specialized disciplines, and the business

Trends In Outsourcing

The concept of externally-funded projects will continue to grow thanks to the increase in
- International competition
- Market globalization
- Global standardization of businesses
- Desire to decrease the cost of deliverables

This environment will ultimately foster an increase in the number of
- Virtual team projects
- Global projects

Figure 2

motivations to decrease the cost of project deliverables. The net result of all of these developments is that there has been a significant increase in the number of virtual team projects, and in the number of global projects, as the response to the growth in outsourcing. (Figure 1-2)

Advancements in project management practices, in formulation of the Work Breakdown Structure (WBS), in formalized planning of projects, in estimating of projects, and in change-management practices for projects, has made it possible, and even convenient, to outsource projects in most industries and in most disciplines. Because of the relative ease of the outsourcing process, it has become acceptable for a significant number of client organizations to outsource a major portion of their deliverable-based work, and even their service-oriented work. Deliverable-based contracts outline a specific deliverable that will have to be presented to the client organization within a desired time frame. The service-oriented portion of a contract will engage a certain number of the performing organization's staff, and physical resources, toward the ongoing activities of the client such as production, operation, maintenance, or security.

Technical Contents of Externally-Funded Projects

- Deliverable-Based Projects
    - Design
        - IT
        - Civil and Structural
        - Process Specialties
        - Industrial and Aerospace
    - Development and Implementation Projects
        - IT
        - System and Software
        - Construction
        - Manufacturing
        - Industrial and Aerospace
        - Design

- Service-Oriented Projects
    - Security
        - IT, System, and Software
        - Physical and Plant
            Office Operations
            Industrial and Manufacturing
    - Maintenance and Operations
        - IT, System, Software
        - Physical and Plant
            Office Operations
            Industrial and Manufacturing

Figure 3

Outsourcing is common for IT development projects, facilities design, physical infrastructure construction, and for ongoing operations such as security and maintenance. Examples of the deliverable-based projects include design and construction of buildings, highways, and bridges. Other outsourced deliverable-based projects could include designing and fabricating computer hardware, software systems, transportation vehicles, and communication hardware. Examples of the contents of service-oriented contracts/projects are plant security, software security, IT maintenance, and facilities maintenance. (Figure 1-3)

An outsourced contract might include both deliverable-based portions and service-oriented portions. The combination of deliverable-based tasks and service-oriented activities is often described as programs in project management literature. However, following the notion that contracts always result in projects, typically service-oriented activities and deliverable-based projects are all bundled together and referred to as projects in the outsourcing community. This practice is reinforced by the fact that the service portion of the contract is not always explicitly highlighted

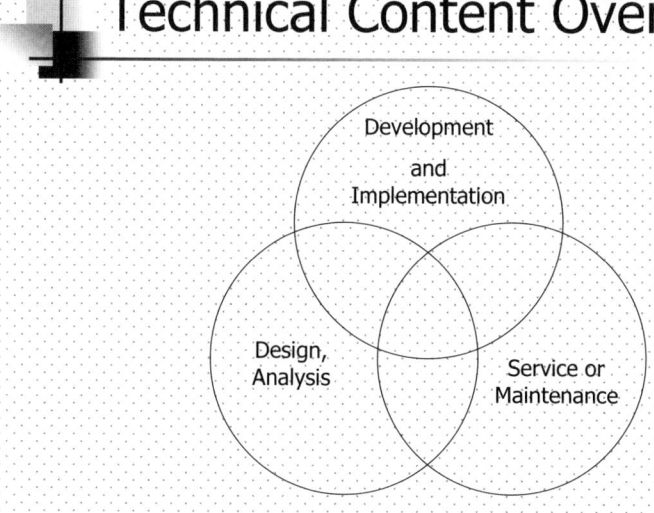

Figure 4

as such in the requests for proposal documents, or in contract documents. Further, there can be overlaps between the usage and implied meanings of the terminology that is used to describe the service-oriented and deliverable-based elements of the major categories of contracts. When there has been a need to highlight the service-oriented portion of the contract, the service-oriented portion of the outsourced work is sometimes called a level-of-effort contract. (Figure 1-4)

An internally-funded project will be initiated when the parent organization, hopefully using sophisticated portfolio management tools, determines that this project is more deserving of funding than all others that have been recommended for funding. Some of the project-oriented organizations employ a prioritization schema, and a formalized prioritization model, in order to compile a ranked list of the most relevant internal projects. Although the formality of this schema varies depending on the project management sophistication of the organization, the project selection rationale is almost always extracted from the strategic and financial objectives of the organization, which are in turn rooted in profits. The connection between the deliverable of an internally-funded project and the strategic objectives, or financial objectives, or the profit, might appear to be subtle and indirect; partly because this connection is usually not explicitly highlighted in the project authorization documents. Nonetheless, the criteria that create a project would hopefully be the same ones that guide the prioritization activities of the portfolio management team during midstream project and portfolio reviews. In other words, the same relevance test that was used during the authorization process should be used during the midstream evaluation.

Somewhat similar to internally-funded projects, the rationale of the performing organization for selecting an externally-funded project is founded on a prioritization schema, and a prioritization model. However, the elements of the selection model are different for externally-funded and internally-funded categories of projects. In the case of externally-funded projects, the selection rationale is directly connected to higher profits, and the selection model explicitly reflects that fact. To put the issues in proper perspective, the success of proposal, and the success of the resulting project, is directly rooted in profits. Naturally, the selection process for an externally-funded project is also based on the probability of securing the intended contract.

The award of the contract by the client organization is guided by yet another prioritization schema. The elements of the schema for the client organization's model in selecting a prospective contractor are entirely different from the ones used by the performing organization in selecting internally-funded or externally-funded projects. Once all of the proposals have been received and reviewed by the client organization, and once the most responsive proposal has been identified, the prospective externally-funded project will become an entity by virtue of the award of a contract from the client organization to the performing organization.

The objectives of the internally-funded projects are either the improvement of a specific operational capability, or the implementation of new process, or the installation of a new deliverable. Internally-funded projects can also be for new product development, or its precursor which is research. In internally-funded projects, the issues that are critical are: value of the deliverable to the organization,

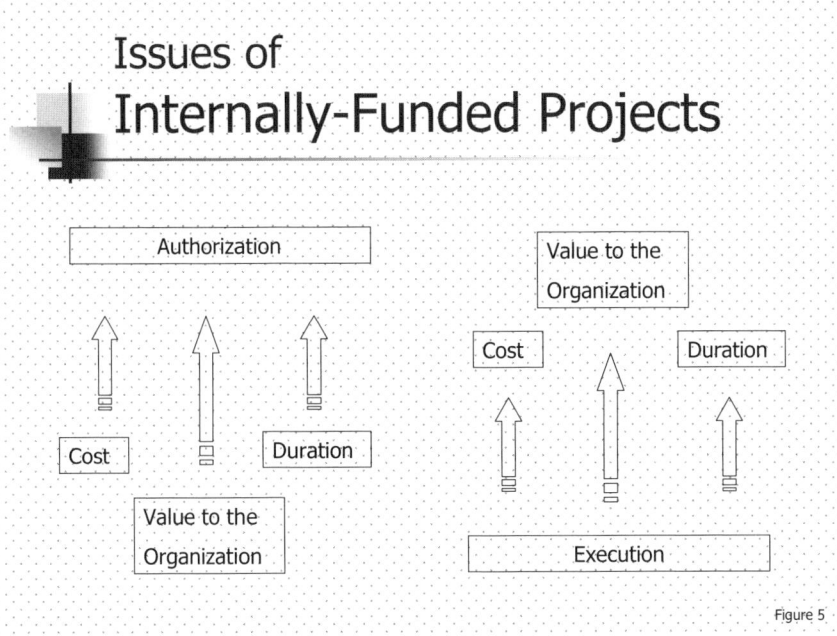

Figure 5

and the general cost-schedule performance of the project. The occasions of criticality are during the admittance of the project into the portfolio, and during the midstream evaluation of the portfolio. The success of the projects will be judged in the light of the business objective that created the project, i.e., capability enhancement and improvements in operations, albeit the intended improvements or capabilities could be subtle and not easily quantifiable in many organizations. The evaluation of cost and duration of internally-funded projects is often diffused, particularly since many internal projects tend to continue to get funded in spite of cost over-runs, if the deliverable continues to appear attractive to the organization. The net result is that the value of the deliverable, and the cost of providing that value, is not always quantifiable. (Figure 1-5)

In the case of an externally-funded project, it is the client that receives the benefit of, and the value from, deliverable in the areas of meeting strategic and financial objectives and performance enhancement. The value of the deliverable of an externally-funded project to the performing organization is primarily the profit that

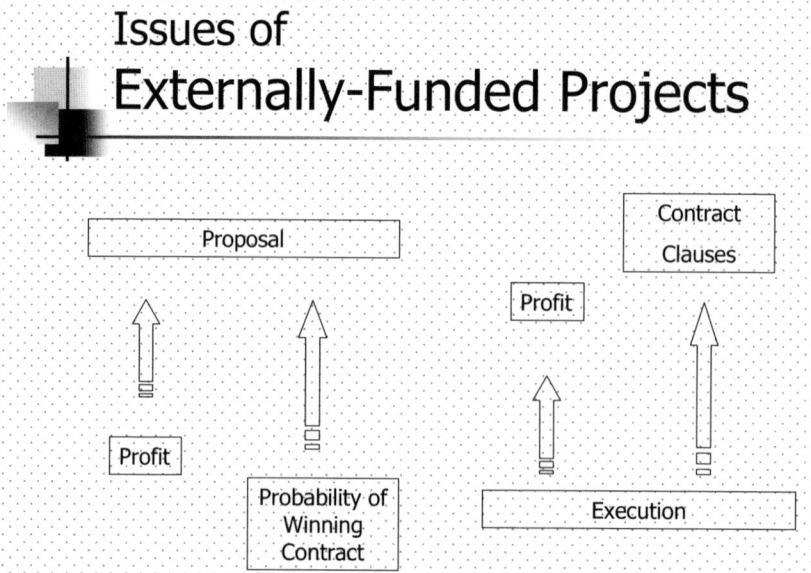

Figure 6

the project, and its associated contract, will contribute to the organization. Usually, this profit is distinct, measurable, and somewhat precise. The issues that become more critical during the selection, and during execution, of externally-funded projects are the contractual and legal obligations, and the immediate profit resulting from the contract/project. (Figure 1-6)

There can be other subtle differences between the environments of organizations that conduct externally-funded projects and organizations that conduct internally-funded projects. The authorization, funding, monitoring, and change-management, of externally-funded projects require extensive documents. Usually, these documents are highlighted in detail in the proposal, and in the contract documents once the project/contract is awarded. Additionally, these projects require legally-formalized reviews and approvals during the change-management process. By comparison, internally-funded projects tend to follow far less legalistic processes, even if the organization employs formalized documentation of plans during the approval process, and even if the organization employs detailed guidelines for reviewing the project status during the change-management process.

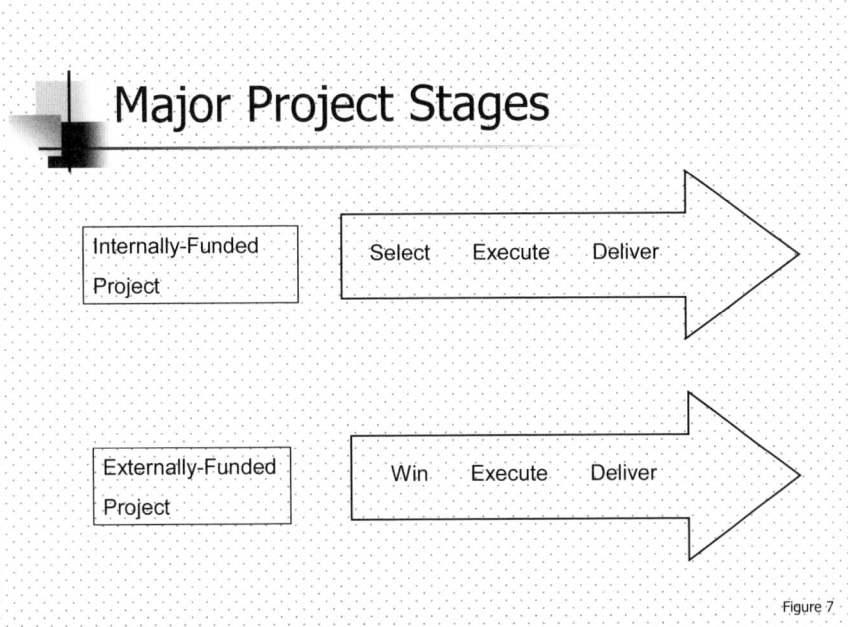

Figure 7

Another significant difference between the internally-funded and externally-funded categories of projects is that an internally-funded project is authorized through a selection process whose mission is to fund the most strategically promising project, whereas an externally-funded project is won as part of a bidding process, during which the performing organization is deemed to be the most qualified, and most responsive, among those who submitted proposals for this project.

However, from the vantage point of the project manager, managing the project in and of itself should be the same, and independent of the source of funding, primarily because the ultimate objective of the project is to craft a specified deliverable. Thus, the commonality among all projects is that, in order to deliver the expected results, the project must be planned in detail, staffed properly, executed gracefully, and managed skillfully. (Figure 1-7)

In performing organizations, there are two distinct functions as they relate to a project that is created as a result of the contract: contract management, and project management. In all likelihood, the manager of an externally-funded project will

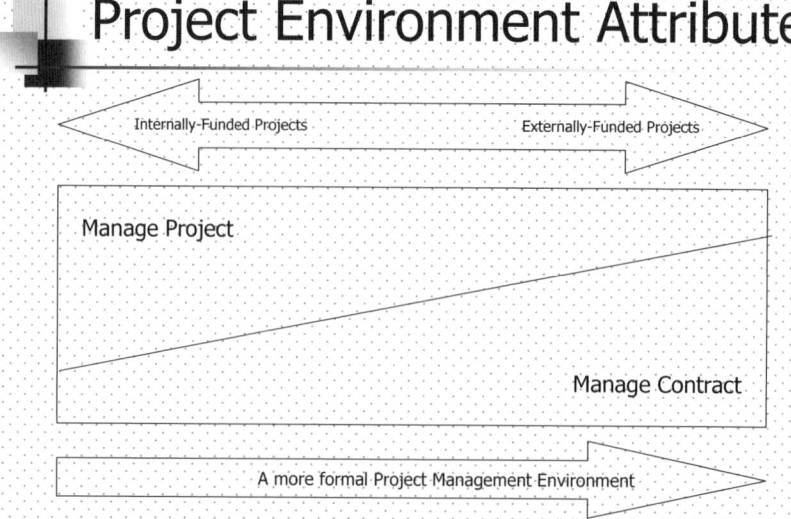

Figure 8

spend relatively more energy managing the administrative and legal issues of the contract than managing the project, whereas the manager of an internally-funded project will spend relatively more energy managing the project, and far less energy managing the administrative issues of the project. It is an ongoing debate as to whether the manager of an externally-funded project should shape the team's activities in the light of contract clauses or in the light of project plans. Sometimes, in performing organizations, the management of the contract is delegated to a contract officer, so that the project manager will be able to concentrate on traditional project management activities. However, in most cases, the project manager performs the duties of the contract officer also. (Figure 1- 8)

1.1 Nomenclature

In organizations where most of the projects are internally-funded, the nomenclature for describing the lifecycle phases of the externally-funded and internally-funded project are fundamentally the same, and independent of the source of funding for the project. This viewpoint, although accurate, tends to sidestep the nature of the contract that creates the externally-funded project. However, if the organization conducts a large number of externally funded projects, business development and contractual issues will gradually temper and influence the terminology that is used in project documents. The distinction between the two mindsets is the insertion of business development activities into traditional project phases of initiating, planning, executing, changing, and closeout.

The first intense business development period is the proposal development period, which occurs during the initiation phase or during the planning phase, depending on the nature of the contract. The next contractually-charged period occurs during the monitoring and change-order periods. Finally, during the closeout phase of the project, the project team and the proposal team must balance an aggressive pursuit of the payments for this project's work, and the efforts in creating a goodwill relationship with the client in order to facilitate securing other projects from the client. It would be fair to say that during the entire project life-cycle, the proposal team and the project team are keenly aware of the contractual tone of the project. (Figure 1-9)

Externally-Funded Project Phases

- Externally funded projects roughly follow the same processes as do internal projects, although the processes are tempered by the existence of business development efforts and contracts
  - Initiation
    - *Proposal*
    - *Contract*
  - Planning
    - *Proposal*
    - *Contract*
  - Execution
    - *Performance and Monitoring*
    - *Contract Modification*
  - Monitoring and Control
    - *Contract Change Orders*
    - *Contract Modification*
  - Close Out
    - *Delivery*
    - *Future Project Award Considerations*

Figure 9

The members of the proposal development team are probably the individuals that are most intensely involved with the business aspects of a project/contract. Therefore, from the vantage point of this team, the project lifecycle phases should include components that would assist in complying with client's wishes for this project, and it should also include features that are designed to improve the likelihood of obtaining another contract from the same client and from other clients within the same industry. Thus, given the contractual environment that surrounds an externally-funded project, not only all project/contract activities will have to conform to project management best practices, but sometimes the planning and reporting documents will also need to be consistent with, and compliant to, the terminology used in contractual clauses. The change in nomenclature will facilitate the planning and orchestration of the project activities in order to facilitate maximum communication between the proposal team and the project team, thus improving the organizational efficiency of the performing organization, particularly as it relates to proposal development pipeline and the resulting profit.

Thus, to carry the contractual tone one step further, and looking at the project strictly from the vantage point of the contract officer, the five phases of the contract/project can be characterized as proposal, contract, performance, contract modification, and delivery. In this view of the project, the legal and contractual aspects clearly overshadow the project management functions. It is an important point that although the phases of an externally-funded project are recited in contractual terms, these phases continue to include all of the features of the traditional project phases. The project phases do not have a one to one correspondence to the contract phases, although there is a significant amount of overlap between the two, and they tend to generally track with each other. (Figure 1-10)

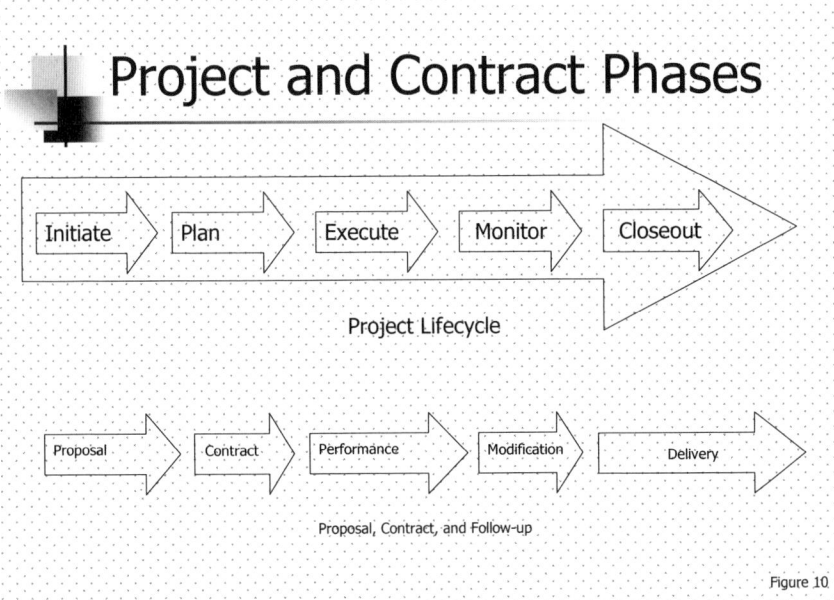

Figure 10

There is no question that traditional project functions will have to be performed in order to deliver products and services to the client. However, using the contractual viewpoint, the project phases, and project management nomenclature, do not take the limelight; the contractual phases and contractual nomenclature do. Further, one can define the project sub-phases in a manner that best highlights the contractual aspects of the project more explicitly and far more emphatically.

The proposal phase might include the activities that are necessary to respond to incremental requests from the client organization for information. These incremental requests are intended to reduce the efforts of the performing organizations in responding to the requests of the client organization, and to lighten the client organization's efforts in creating a smaller and more appropriate bidder pool. Request for Qualification is usually a solicitation for verifiable information about the competency and track record of the resources of the prospective performing organization. Request for Quotation is usually for portions of the project that do not require an extensive proposal, just the bid price. Some organizations open the bids in a public forum, and in the presence of most of the bidders, while others open the proposals and bids without the presence of any of the proposing organizations. Lastly, some organizations hold meetings with a few of the top-ranked prospective contractors in order to clarify proposal and contractual issues and possibly negotiate the values of cost and duration elements. The results of these meetings will provide the final pieces of information that might be necessary to define the project goals more clearly. The meetings will also provide other information that might be pivotal to identifying one of the proposing organizations as the most qualified for the forthcoming project.

Once the contract is awarded to a performing organization, the contractor will promptly marshal all necessary resources to start the execution of the project. The next contractually intense period will be when the progress reports, and requests for progress payments, are submitted to the client for processing incremental payments for the project work. Progress payments are reimbursements of actual expenditures, and the corresponding fee, that is due the contractor for the work done up to that point; not only for cost-plus projects but sometimes for lump-sum projects also. For lump-sum projects, although there is a pre-fixed price for the deliverable, some client organizations entertain requests for incremental payments toward the price of the contract on the basis of the delivered portion of the work. These incremental payments are usually predicated by a definitive measure of the fraction of the deliverable that has been produced by the contractor.

It is during this period that change-orders might be submitted to the client organization requesting additional payment for work/deliverable that might not have been specified in the contract, but became necessary during the project execution. If the additional charges, commonly known as claims, are rejected by the client, there would be back-charges as part of payments. Back-charges are mechanisms by which the client organization disallows a certain item contained in the request for payment document. Independent of these payment issues, the final phase of the contract will include a formal delivery of the project results, project closeout, and financial closeout of the project charges. If there are any outstanding

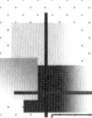

Externally-Funded Project Phases
From the Contracting Officer's Vantage Point

- **Proposal Phase**
  - Request for Qualifications
  - Request for Quotation
  - Request for Proposal
  - Bid opening
  - Prospective Contractor Meeting

- **Contract Phase**
  - Contract Negotiations
  - Contract Award

- **Performance Phase**
  - Mobilization
  - Execution

- **Contract Modification Phase**
  - Progress reports
  - Progress payments
  - Change orders
  - Back charges
  - Claims

- **Delivery Phase**
  - Final delivery
  - Closeout
  - Plans for future follow-on work
  - Back charges
  - Claims
  - Litigation

Figure 11

charges, or back-charges, at that point the stage is set for possible distasteful tasks of repeated and multiple contractual claims and litigation, that might have started midstream during the project, and might continue or even intensify after the project has been completed (Figure 1- 11)

Various efforts in the areas of partnering have provided a non-confrontational contract environment, but the fact remains that contractor organizations and client organizations have two entirely different sets of motivations and objectives. In a contracting situation, the contractor/bidder's objectives are to win the contract, a speedy completion of the project, prompt payment, and a good profit. On the other hand, the client's objectives are to pay the lowest price possible, for the earliest delivery date, and for the most responsive performance.

There are circumstances that teams from these two categories of organizations collaborate harmoniously, and create a cordial environment. Nonetheless, the organizational loyalty and administrative attachment is always at the forefront of the consciousness of the staff members who are involved in these activities. The number of lawsuits that clients and contractors file against one another demonstrates this possible underlying adversarial attitude, which stems from the disparity between client's business objectives and contractor's operating objectives.

Chapter Summary Contracts are part of the business landscape of many organizations, albeit sometimes an organization might be the client organization of the project, while at other times it might be the performing organization of the contract. Performing organizations tend to place a noticeable importance on the contract, relative to the accompanying project, as symbolized by the use of contractual nomenclature to describe the project phases. Consequently, often project managers not only will have to manage the project, but they also have to manage the contractual agreements of the project.

2. Proposal Phase

Organizations that serve as contractors and subcontractors to external clients regard proposal management units as one of the most valuable units of the organization, possibly the single most valuable unit. The proposal management unit of a performing organization will greatly influence whether or not the enterprise will thrive toward operational excellence, and toward higher profits. This organizational unit has the mission of efficiently engaging in proposal prospect forecasting, and managing the activities that are involved in converting a prospect into a contract.

A well-structured proposal management unit will generate creative strategic options to capture emerging opportunities, and will implement proposal strategies that achieve the desired financial goals. A sophisticated proposal management unit would apply the latest concepts and methods in selection and pursuance of new business prospects, in accordance with the articulated wishes of the upper executives, of course. The prerequisite of this process is that the organization must have clear strategies for business goals, and a detailed proposal development agenda.

The proposal development process should be considered not a sporadic temporary activity, but rather an integral component of the business strategy. Preparing a proposal should be based on a deliberate strategic decision, and based on focusing the organization's precious resources toward areas of highest reward potential. To that end, the proposal management unit will optimize the proposal mix with resources allocation, with profits, and with risks inherent in the contracting process. Formalized proposal development processes will assist the streamlined selection of the most appropriate and suitable projects, in order to sustain a competitive advantage for the organization.

Success ingredients of the proposal process are the existence of mechanisms that will allow the proposal team, and by extension the resulting proposal, to respond to the competitive pressures of the environment of a particular prospective contract. Further, in sophisticated project performing organizations, the proposal management unit designs and implements continuously-improved processes for managing the proposal development pipeline.

An organizational environment is more likely to produce successful proposals if the organization provides a facilitative environment for the proposal team members. Characteristics of a facilitative environment are the presence of a comprehensive set of best practices, a collection of lessons-learned, a fully established data-archiving schema, and accessible tools for retrieval of historical data. The infrastructure would include prospect identification tools, prospect prioritization tools, access to technical expertise, sufficient supply of people resources and equipment resources, and ample funding. It is only then that the team will be capable of analyzing the dynamic external business environment in order to detect new opportunities.

Just like project management, formality and repeatability constitute the essence of sophistication in proposal development. The benefits of a formalized proposal system can be noticed in improvements in productivity of the proposal team in developing the proposal, and in the productivity of the project team in executing the resulting project. Formality of processes will also promote employee morale, satisfaction of the internal client, and ultimately in the satisfaction of the external client, as derived from the project's results.

The sophistication of the proposal development process can be inferred from competency of the members of the proposal team, the harmony of proposal teams, productivity of proposal teams, friendliness of the enterprise towards proposals, and the level of support and facilitation that is available to the proposal team by the parent organization. Further, an enlightened organization will foster extensive communication among the proposal team, the project team, the internal client, and the external client

The credibility, accuracy, and the completeness of the proposal will be highly enhanced if the team members had expertise in all of the disciplines that are related to the business environment, project management, and in the full spectrum of the technical content of the prospective project. Since it is somewhat unrealistic to expect one small team to have expertise in all of these areas, and for all possible projects, the proposal management unit should form a proposal team that is specific to each proposal, the membership of which will come from the appropriate specialty disciplines that are impacted by the prospective project. Thus, as the circumstances warrant, the proposal team's expertise will extend into the areas of management, finance, engineering, technology, information systems, manufacturing, assembly, marketing, management, production planning, IT, engineering, operations, business development, purchasing, contracting, and financial management. (Figure 2-1)

Proposal Preparation Team

- Proposal Writer
- Financial Expert
- Marketing Professional
- Business Developer
- Account Executive
- Contract Expert
- Project Planner
- Project Estimator
- Project Manager
- Product Manager
- Departmental Manager
- Executive Management

- Engineering
- Technology
- Information Systems
- Manufacturing
- Assembly
- Production
- Information Technology

Figure 1

The proposal preparation team should be as all-inclusive as possible in order to maximize the responsiveness and comprehensiveness of the proposal. Thus, the proposal team should include the prospective project manager, some of the prospective team members, and representatives form the project management office. In turn, during the execution phase of the project, the proposal management unit should be apprised of the progress of the contract/project for the benefit of the contract at hand and, equally importantly, for the benefit of future contracts from the same client or from similar clients. Therefore, the project teams and proposal teams should be in continuous communication with one another, albeit sometimes the proposal team is the predominant membership while in other times the project team is the predominant membership. (Figure 2-2)

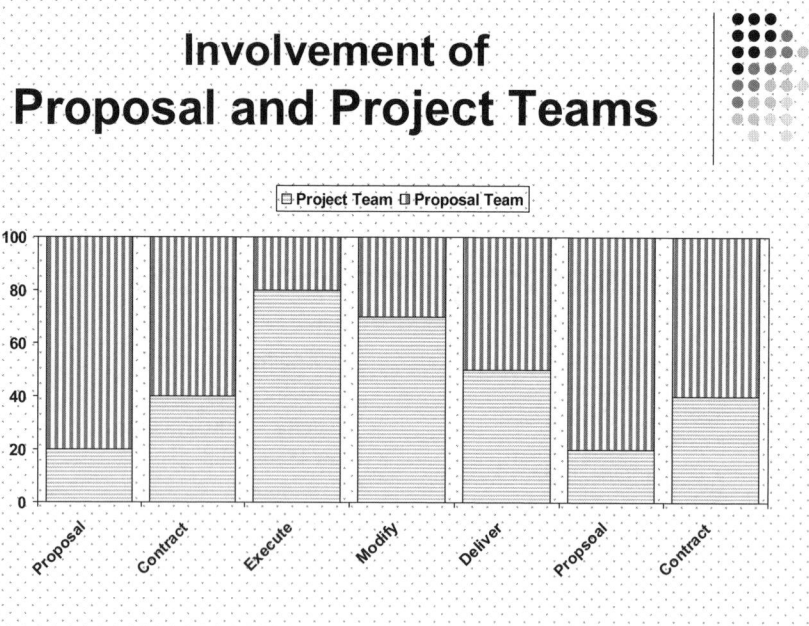

Figure 2

A successful proposal management unit will make available best practices and guidelines for comprehensively managing things issues, people issues, and enterprise issues. Things issues are those that deal with inanimate objects such as forms, models, calculations, extrapolations, and data capture tools. Within the context of proposals, they refer to processes and procedures for issues such as handling prospect identification, prospect prioritization, and proposal development. People issues deal with interrelationships and performance of the people involved in the overall business development process, and specifically in drafting a responsive and successful proposal. Within the context of proposals, the people issues refer to processes, and facilitative environment, for individual competency assessment, and for professional growth. People issues also refer to skills in dealing with people who are within the parent organization and outside the parent organization. Given that there is an overlap between the proposal team and the project team, the people issues will include those attributes that make both categories of these teams communicative, harmonious, productive, and cohesive. Probably the most illusive of the issues that would need to be addressed as part of the proposal management process are the enterprise issues. Enterprise issues deal with organizational culture, organizational mission, organizational capabilities, organizational strategic direction, organizational infrastructure, and an underlying continuous-improvement culture. (Figure 2- 3)

Components of a Successful Proposal development System

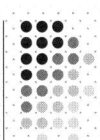

- Things-Related Issues
  - Prospect identification tools
  - Source identification procedures
  - Prioritization model
  - Indices of the prioritization model
  - Response generation
  - Streamlined proposal development
  - Proposal quality management
  - Solicitation of follow-on work

- People-Related Issues
  - Individual current technical skills
  - Individual skill development plan
  - Teamwork skills and processes
  - Team competency plan
  - Relationship management

- Enterprise-Related Issues
  - Proposal development processes
  - Work environment
  - Support systems
  - Organizational strategies
  - Organizational quality management
  - Organizational competency enhancement
  - Continuous improvement

Figure 3

In the case of internally-funded projects, project selection and project initiation are performed on the basis of parameters that are generally internal to the organization. The selection and initiation processes involve a prioritization process whose objective is to select a few projects from among all projects that might have been proposed by the various divisions of the organization.

By contrast, there are two series of prioritizations that govern the creation of an externally-funded project. The first prioritization is conducted in the performing organization in order to select the potential projects for which the performing organization would wish to prepare proposals and bids; this is sometimes called prospect prioritization or opportunity prioritization. This prioritization is, implicitly or explicitly, based on profits and technical compatibility.

The second prioritization is conducted by the client organization in order to select, partly on the basis of the proposals and partly based on the likelihood of the success of the prospective contractor, the most qualified contractor for this project. The selection is performed through a prioritization process that compares the proposals that have been submitted from several potential contractors for the same deliverable. The performing organization that is selected is commonly referred to as the most qualified bidder, and hence the winner of the contract.

The rationale of the prioritization that is conducted at the client organization will typically be based on the prospective project's total cost and duration, as proposed by the performing organization. The prioritization schema of the client organization would also have evaluative elements that give consideration to the likelihood of success of a given contractor. The likelihood of success of the proposing organization is inferred from the prospective contractor's performance history, and from its perceived project management sophistication. Some client organizations rely on the verified project management maturity rating of the proposing organization in order to predict the success of the forthcoming project.

2.1 Proposal Steps

The proposal development processes can be grouped into three major steps: identify prospects, prioritize the prospect data, and prepare the proposal. The identification step includes the efforts for compiling a comprehensive list of all those client organizations whose projects are slated to be outsourced, and thus they are currently seeking performing organizations for those projects. The next step would involve isolating those prospective projects that represent a high technical compatibility with the performing organization's specialty, and those prospective projects that have the potential for a healthy profit. Having prepared a short list of proposals, each proposal will receive the attention and effort that it deserves in order to be responsive, and outstanding among the client's bidder pool. Ideally, the process of making a selective list of prospective projects/contracts from the original lengthy list should be formalized, and explicitly constructed upon the long-term strategies, and immediate objectives, of the performing organization. (Figure 2- 4)

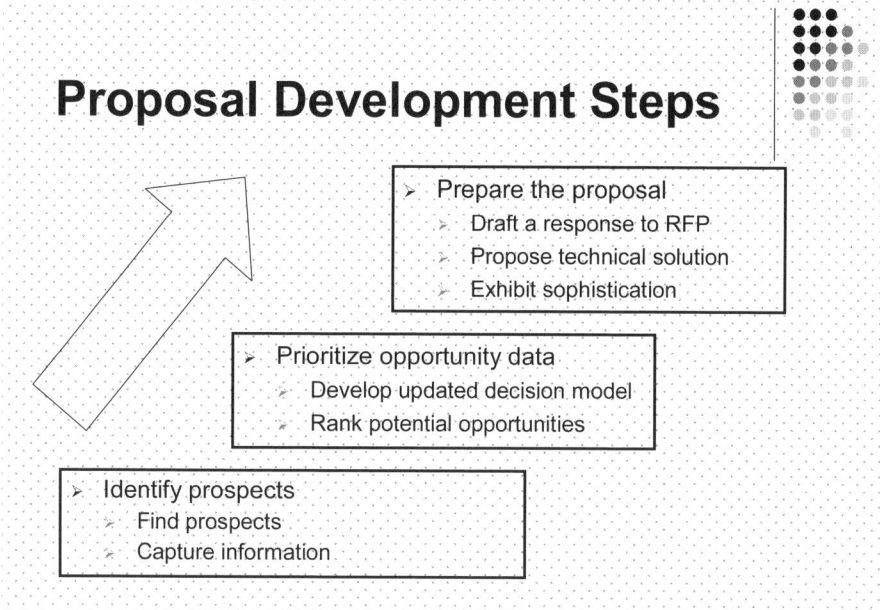

Figure 4

Proposal Phase 24

Sometimes, the first indication of a possible contract is an official or an unofficial notification that the proposing organization might receive from any one of its marketing efforts, trade shows, advertising, referrals, customers, direct mail, telemarketing and networking. However, a formalized proposal development process would start with the identification and cataloging of the potential proposal prospects, hopefully on a uniform and repeatable basis. The identification of prospects should not be treated as an ad-hoc process; rather all sources of information should be queried on a regular basis. Additionally, the data elements that are collected through this process should be deliberately selective. Many of the information clearinghouses have an electronic outlet for their information. Thus, the collection of the data from these sources can easily be accomplished through the internet, automatically, seamlessly, and methodically. (Figure 2- 5)

Identify Prospects

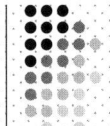

- ➢ Find prospects from
    - ➢ Federal government
    - ➢ State and local government
    - ➢ Private sector
    - ➢ International entities
- ➢ Capture information on
    - ➢ Client
    - ➢ Project contents of the contract
    - ➢ Competitors
        - ➢ Population
        - ➢ Capabilities, individual and average

Figure 5

Data should be collected on the organizational features of the prospective client, the technical contents of the prospective project, and the nature of competitive environment that is likely to exist for a specific project. The two major elements of the competitive environment are the size of the competitive pool, and the sophistication of the organizations that are likely to submit competing proposals towards this prospective project. These two elements will determine the flexibility that the performing organization will have in setting the profit margin for the project. In cases of intense competition, the performing organization will have to spend more effort in proposal preparation in order to be the winner, even though the anticipated profit might have to be set to a lower value. Accordingly, the size of the potential bidder pool is one of the important indices of the model that prioritizes the prospects, or a significant item of debate in organizations that select prospects through debates. A checklist can be used in the process of collecting information that will be used for for assessing the nature of the competitive environment. (Figure 2- 6)

Proposal Competition
Checklist

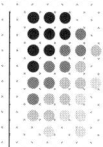

- How many organizations are likely to bid on this project
- Who are, or could be, our competitors?
- Have any of them reacted to this proposal?
- What do we anticipate to be the competitors bid?
- How detailed should our plans be?
- What profit margin will be appropriate for this proposal?
- What additional information do we need for drafting the proposal?

Figure 6

Many proposal teams, and proposal management units, find that the rationale for selecting a prospect over another to be difficult to quantify, sometimes even difficult to verbalize. Therefore, in many contractor organizations, the prioritization of proposal prospects becomes a task for the upper executives, who will conduct extensive debates in order to arrive at the short list of the potentially most viable proposals. This mode of operation is rather short-sighted because it renders the prioritization process ad-hoc, continually evolving, and highly personality-based.

A formalized model that addresses all of the relevant and important issues would streamline the prioritization process. The existence of the model, even a rudimentary one, will prompt the proposal team to verbalize and quantify the various elements that are deemed to be important to the upper executives. Further, the existence of the model would facilitate a structured debate on all of the contributing issues, that ultimately would lead to the continuous improvement of the model itself. The net result is that a formalized process would assure that all of the leads would go through a consistent process for prioritization and possible

Prioritize Opportunity Data

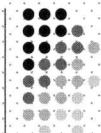

- ➤ Develop and update formalized prioritization model to include
    - ➤ Company's strategic plan
    - ➤ Specialty areas
    - ➤ Track record
    - ➤ Probability of winning the contract
    - ➤ Estimate of the profit from the potential contract
    - ➤ Likelihood of locating internal resources for key positions
    - ➤ Convenient access to qualified subcontractors for this project
- ➤ Rank potential opportunities in the light of
    - ➤ Importance of these indices
    - ➤ Values of these indices

Figure 7

follow-up. Consequently, the proposal team will know much more clearly when to abandon a lead, and when to follow a lead aggressively. Probably the most significant side-effect of the implementation of a formalized prioritization process is that it would free the upper executives from the obligation of attending the debate meetings. (Figure 2-7)

Using a WBS-like structure for the characterization and quantification of the importance of prospective projects, these projects can be compared and prioritized on a consistent basis. Although the model can grow to become highly complex, the first attempt could be to develop a model containing the three major categories of importance, namely technical compatibility, strategic issues, and financial issues. Through such an approach, the proposal team will have at its disposal a tool with which the team can explicitly assign different degrees of importance to the technical compatibility, strategic importance, and financial importance, of the prospective contract/project. To carry that one step further, the team can assign different degrees of importance to profit margin, cash flow, competitive issues of the project, and compatibility of the organizational technical expertise with project content.

Naturally, the list of indices is fully expected to be different for each organization, and in line with that organization's strategic missions. The scoring points that are assigned to each index are quantitative indications of the importance of each particular index to the organization. Therefore, it is a significant issue that another organization might assign entirely different points of importance to their indices, even if the organization uses the same suite of indices. The total number of possible points that a project can achieve is 100. Thus, on the basis of the objectives of the mythical organizational illustrated here, technical compatibility has a weight of 20 points, the strategic issues have a weight of 40, and the financial issues have a weight of 40. The project shown in this example scored 15/20 points for the technical compatibility, 30/40 points for the strategic importance of the deliverable, and 24/40 points for the financial implications of the project deliverable. Thus, the total score for this mythical project is 69/100. Having this scoring data available for each project, the prioritization of the prospective projects will be completed by preparing a list of the projects as ranked by their earned points as derived from this model. It is an important point that the absolute values of the total score of projects are not nearly as important as are the relative values that are calculated for a group of projects that are in the pool of potential projects/proposals. (Figure 2-8)

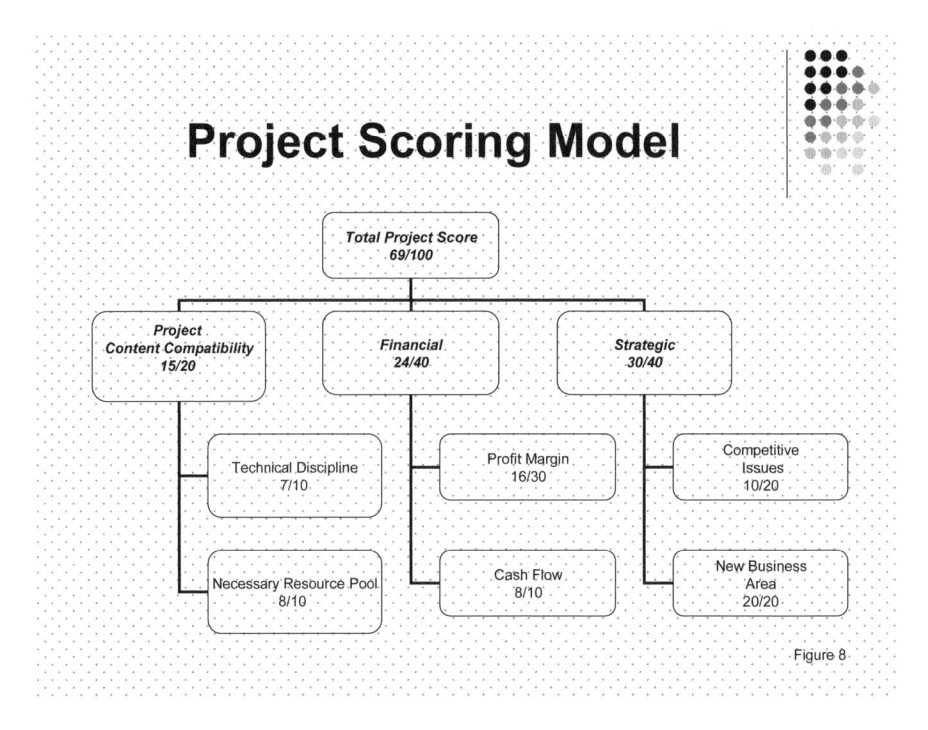

Project Scoring Model

- Total Project Score: 69/100
  - Project Content Compatibility: 15/20
    - Technical Discipline: 7/10
    - Necessary Resource Pool: 8/10
  - Financial: 24/40
    - Profit Margin: 16/30
    - Cash Flow: 8/10
  - Strategic: 30/40
    - Competitive Issues: 10/20
    - New Business Area: 20/20

Figure 8

Once the number of potential prospects has been reduced to a manageable value, then the proposal team can concentrate on developing a timely, sophisticated, and responsive, proposal for each prospective project. With a small and focused number of projects/proposals, the proposal teams can concentrate on the specifics of each project far more efficiently. Thus, each proposal team can prepare their respective proposal in a manner that it will include meaningful and contractually-appropriate responses to the administrative portion of the proposal request. More importantly, the proposal team will have the opportunity to propose a more focused and a more suitable deliverable for the client; one that will help this proposing organization stand out among all other proposing organizations.

An enlightened organization will have information about the client organization's project environment, and detailed knowledge of what will best work for a specific client. Thus, an informed proposal team will be able to craft a proposal that meets the objectives of the client very closely. Additionally, the proposal team should demonstrate the performing organization's superlative capabilities by showing an awareness of the full spectrum of the issues surrounding the proposal's subject matter. The trademark of a sophisticated proposal development team is to extend beyond simply meeting the minimum, and the stated, objectives of the request for proposal documents, and the obvious requirements of the contract. Rather, the proposal should advance a solution that surpasses those objectives. In this context, surpassing does not mean proposing something other than what the client had envisioned, but rather proposing a more informed solution that meets the objectives more gracefully and more directly than described in the request for proposal. The premise is that, although the client organization's approach might be reasonable, sometimes the unique vantage point of the proposing organization might afford its technical experts the opportunity to craft a different, and possibly more direct,

Prepare the Proposal

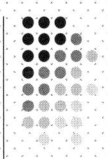

- Draft a responsive proposal document containing
  - Requested technical material
  - Requested administrative material
- Propose a technical solution
  - Meet the basic intent of the client
  - Exceed the expectations by advancing an innovative solution
- Exhibit sophistication by
  - Listing assumptions
  - Taking exceptions
  - Making suggestions

Figure 9

solution to the problem that the deliverable is intended to address. To sum up, a stellar proposal is one that clearly establishes the proposing organization as a progressive, sophisticated, dynamic, and appropriate organization for the forthcoming project. (Figure 2-9)

Ideally, all of the proposal development efforts will be facilitated and orchestrated by a central organizational unit which is commissioned to provide facilitation for the proposal development teams. To that end, the proposal management unit must establish, define, and implement, a sophisticated and effective review process for the activities of the proposal management unit, and specifically for all of the three steps of the proposal development process. The purpose of such a process is to select tools and processes that support and facilitate the organizational proposal development effort in the most efficient manner. If the organization already has a full-function EPMO in place, the proposal management unit can become a constituent component of the EPMO.

It would be fully expected from a sophisticated organization to have a process enhancement initiative in place. The efforts for enhancement of the proposal development process should utilize metrics that monitor, quantify, and evaluate the effectiveness of the proposal development system, and the rate by which this system is improving.

The raw progress data and refined success data should be collected from all of the individual activities of the three steps of the proposal preparation process, i.e., prospect identification, opportunity prioritization, and proposal preparation. The volume and nature of the collected data should clearly characterize all sub-steps of the process: find prospects, capture information, develop updated decision model, rank potential prospects, draft a response, propose a solution, and exhibit sophistication. Accordingly, continuous improvement efforts for proposal development should be focused at the effectiveness of the individual sub-steps of the process. (Figure 2-10)

Enhancements to
Proposal Development Processes

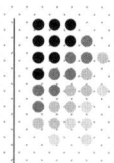

- Identify prospects
  - Find prospects
  - Capture information
- Prioritize opportunity data
  - Develop updated decision model
  - Rank potential prospects
- Prepare the proposal
  - Draft a response to RFP
  - Propose solution
  - Exhibit sophistication

Continuously Monitor and Improve

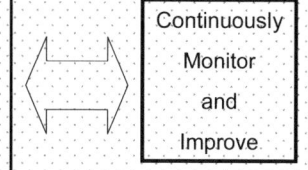

Figure 10

The data elements that can be collected, as indicators of progress and efficiency of the continuous improvement efforts, should be comprehensive enough so that one can determine overall performance characteristics of the proposal development system. Although a vast number of indices can be the subject of this efficiency monitoring process, care must be taken to select enough data to get a picture of the efficiency of the process, but stop short of overwhelming the participants of the proposal development enhancement effort. Performance characteristics should include metrics such as clearly-quantified characterizations of the average expected profit margin from the pipeline, the overall likelihood of winning of contracts, and the total number of proposals currently in the pipeline. Other data to be collected are those that deal with the attributes of the organizational infrastructure that supports the proposal development team, such as the number of people within the team, the number of processes, and the amount of funds, which will be spent for proposal development; per successful project, and annually for all proposals.

Proposal Phase

The historical and current pipeline data can then be used to continuously improve the proposal devotement process, improve the success rate of proposals, and increase the overall profit margin of the organization. Proposal success rate and overall organizational profit margin are somewhat interrelated and improve generally in tandem. Therefore, if insightful data is collected, the discrepancies between the growth of each of these two organizational facets can be identified and analyzed. (Figure 2-11)

The Proposal Pipeline Statistics

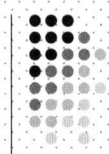

- Average profit of the prospective contracts
- Average likelihood of winning
- Historical average capture ratio
- The portion of contracts that result from recapture
- Number of people writing proposals
- The extent to which the processes are formalized
- Average size, and range of sizes, of proposals
- Total number of proposals in the pipeline
- Winning proposal ratio
- Profit potential of successful proposals
- Proposal development process details
- Proposal development cost
- Proposal development efficiency
  - From resource expenditure standpoint
  - From timeline standpoint
- Return on investment for the proposal development process
- Alignment of contracts with organizational competencies

Figure 11

It is always helpful to summarize data in a manner that is transverse to the normal flow. For example, although it is useful to look at a project from the vantage point of project phases, some issues can be observed more clearly when the same phases are examined within the context of the knowledge areas. Likewise, continuous improvements in the proposal development process would benefit from categorizing the performance data into the areas of management of things issues, people issues, and enterprise issues of the proposals preparation process. The availability of the detailed performance data categorized in this fashion will allow the proposal development team to expand the base of their strength, and to put measures in place to remedy any possible areas of weakness. (Figure 2-12)

Continuous Improvement In The Proposal Processes

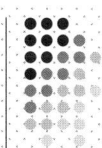

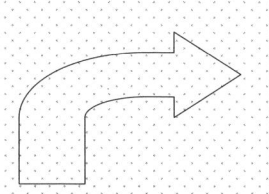

- Achieve excellence in proposal development through in-depth knowledge of
  - General market conditions
  - Focused and sophisticated response to requests for proposal

- Foster improved capabilities for dealing with
  - Things-related issues
  - People-related issues
  - Enterprise-related issues

Figure 12

Detailed proposal pipeline data would provide ample clues for improving the manner in which the performing organization collects data on prospective clients and competitors. In turn, detailed knowledge of the prospective projects will allow the organization to assign the right mix of professionals to the future proposal teams, and by extension, the right mix of professionals for the execution of the future projects. Equally important, a fully-informed view of the proposal pipeline will facilitate the induction of the right professionals to the overall organizational resource pool. Lastly, it will guide the organization in enhancing the infrastructure that will support the proposal team, and the subsequent project team, by the development of formalized models, and the acquisition of operational tools.

2.2 Goals of the Proposed Project

Normally, a proposal would contain almost exactly what the contract would contain, and it is structured the same way also. The contents of the proposal can be divided into two distinct categories: administrative and technical. The administrative portion of the proposal describes the financial, legal, procedural, and infrastructure obligations of the client and performing organizations. Additionally, the administrative portion contains the description of financial consequences of non-conformance with the administrative or technical imperatives of the proposal/contract. By comparison, the technical portion of the proposal describes all of the activities, processes, and equipment, which would need to be employed in order to effectuate the end-result that is desired by the client organization. Typically, the technical portion includes a Statement of Work (SOW), which is a narrative description of the objectives of the service, or the attributes of the deliverable. Sometimes, SOW is followed by a detailed description of the

Proposal Components

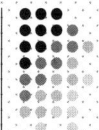

- Legal and administrative clauses of contract
  - Terms and conditions
  - Reporting details
  - Status review meeting processes
  - Management requirements

- *Technical details of the deliverable*
  - *Statement of work*
  - *Narrative specifications*
  - *Graphic drawings*
  - *Tabular data and quantitative attributes*

Figure 13

deliverable/services; in narrative, graphic, and tabular fashion, as appropriate for the project content. (Figure 2-13)

A certain amount of project planning is always conducted during the proposal preparation, which is essentially akin to project initiation phase of an internal project. The proposal phase of a contract is as important to the contract as are the combination of initiation and planning phases of a project to an internally-funded project. It is crucial to have the project planning data as detailed, and as accurate, as possible because an accurate plan of the project/contract will assist the performing organization in developing an informed strategy for developing a price structure for that forthcoming project. Unfortunately, development of a detailed plan for each contract opportunity is highly impracticable, and sometime impossible, due to the limited time and limited information that is available at that phase of the proposal/contract. However, if the organization is sophisticated in the project management discipline, more detailed and credible plans can be developed for the proposed project even if there are limited time and data available for the proposal development phase.

The initial plans, which are developed during the proposal development phase, should address as many of the following attributes of the prospective project as possible, albeit in a rough and tentative form: WBS, cost estimate, master schedule, resource forecasts, and risk management plan. Once the project is authorized, and as the first task of the project, the project team should build on these rough plans in order to develop a set of detailed project plans.

The planning tasks and implementation tasks of an externally-funded project are normally conducted in line with the detailed definition of the scope and objectives of the project as articulated in the technical portion of the contract. The deliverable and performance details are initially outlined in the technical portion of the request for proposal document, and often they tend to become slightly modified as they re-appear in the contract. Depending on the industry and on other variables, the detailed articulation of client's needs and wishes is called objectives, requirements, or specifications. This book uses the term specifications to refer collectively to all three.

It is incumbent upon the client organization to make the specifications as clear as possible. In order to facilitate comprehension of, and compliance with, the specifications of the contract, all facets of the project deliverable must be quantified in the proposal; to the extent practicable, of course. Accordingly, attempts should be made to quantify those deliverable qualifiers that are highly subject to interpretation, such as easy, robust, agile, advanced, modern, capable, speedy, smooth, and aesthetically pleasing. However, if there are ambiguous points in the request for proposal, the proposing organization can use these minor blemishes as opportunities to highlight the performing organization's sophistication, by offering quantified responses to the items in the proposal whose current description in the proposal lacks clarity.

The detailed information for project specifications can be presented in written, tabular, and graphic formats. To some extent, the choice of the format is dictated by the nature of the information. For example, graphic format is most efficient in conveying the arrangement, size, and location of physical components, while spreadsheets and tables would be the venue of choice for portraying numerical relationships. Lastly, text would be most appropriate for depicting verbal description of objectives, activities, performance criteria, and strategic issues.

The specifications documents are the most formalized articulation of the needs and expectations of the client organization. For the deliverable-based portion of the contract, specifications documents usually describe what will be delivered to the client organization once the project is completed. With respect to the desired deliverable or service, the specifications document should include the technical data that is necessary to plan and implement the project, and to conduct the work. Thus, the specifications might have details of materials, equipment, services, procedures, and tools that should be used for the project.

If the project specifications outline the activities of the project without any major emphasis on the deliverables, they would be less useful for the project team, unless the proposal solicitation is for a series of services, and it is only by tradition called a project; or unless the contract environment will be that of a cost-plus-fee environment. For service-oriented portion of the contract, the specifications highlight the activities, and the intensity of resources for those activities, with very little emphasis on a specific deliverable. Some contracting personnel, particularly in the cost-plus and service-oriented environments, regard the expenditure of material resources, the presence of equipment, and the presence of people resources, as deliverables in and of themselves.

The specifications should provide details of all those items or services that are needed or desired. It should also include details of all those deliverable features that are considered undesirable or unacceptable, and those services that are not necessary. Further, the specifications should outline those deliverable items that are necessary for the success of the project but will be fabricated, developed, implemented, or delivered, by the efforts of another project. There are three major types of specifications: focused design, generic performance, and functional.

Focused design, or product, specifications provide details of what is to be delivered either in terms of physical and metaphysical characteristics, or in terms of detailed processes and sequences that are intended to contribute to a product or a service. Most of the specifications for the service-oriented projects fall into the focused design category. An example of this type of specifications is where the client organization provides details of how web pages should be designed, what graphics should be used in the various web pages, where the clipart should be placed, where the links should be placed, and how many records should the database contain. As such, the risk of performance, and the risk of applicability, of the final deliverable, rest directly and solely with the client organization. The performing organization is simply responsible for conformance to the specifications. (Figure 2-14)

Focused Design Specifications

- **Features**
  - Provides extensive and explicit details of the physical characteristics of the deliverable and services

- **Uncertainties**
  - Places the risk of performance, and the risk of applicability, on the client

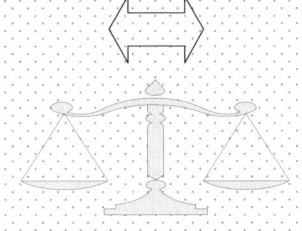

Figure 14.

If the specifications are drafted with generic performance characteristics in mind, they define measurable capabilities that the deliverable must achieve in terms of operational capabilities, but leave some freedom for the performing organization to adopt the best strategy to meet those capabilities. An example of this type of specifications is where the client spells out the access speed, error rate, and general linkage characteristics of the web site. The project team will then draft plans for a deliverable that will have the proper technical features such that the deliverable would satisfy the client organization's performance expectations. In this case, the risk of performance of the deliverable (in the light of the performance specifications) is borne by the performing organization, while the risk of applicability is borne by the client organization. (Figure 2-15)

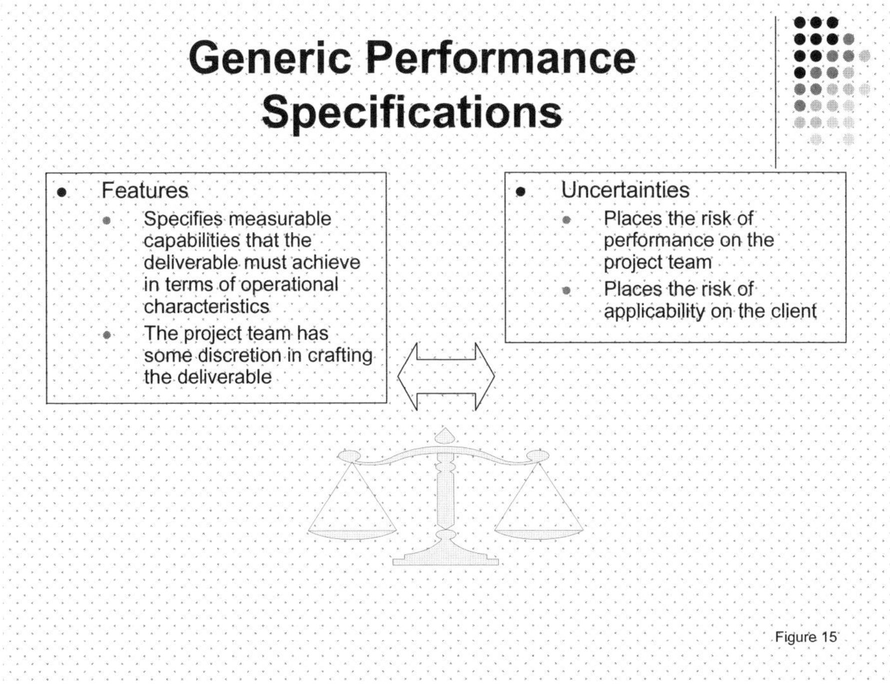

Generic Performance Specifications

- Features
  - Specifies measurable capabilities that the deliverable must achieve in terms of operational characteristics
  - The project team has some discretion in crafting the deliverable

- Uncertainties
  - Places the risk of performance on the project team
  - Places the risk of applicability on the client

Figure 15

A set of functional specifications is the most logical mode of articulating the strategic intention of the client organization, while stopping short of prescribing the means of meeting these strategic intentions. If the client organization uses this philosophy for its specifications, it would simply provide the contractor the general business plan and the expected business outcome. For better or for worse, this form of specifications burdens the client organization with the task of defining, in very clear terms, the basic business objective of the final product, and not the deliverable product itself. In turn, this mode of specification development will empower the creativity of the project team in utilizing innovative techniques to meet or exceed the client's expectations. The performing organization, as the first task of the execution of the project, will develop a set of detailed specifications for a deliverable that, in the judgment of the performing organization, would enable the project to meet those business needs.

Most of the software and system development projects follow this concept, in that the implementation team develops the project specifications after interpreting and analyzing the needs and expectations of the client. Under this mode of specifications development, it is entirely possible that the project manager will communicate the specifications to the client organization, but that is usually just to keep the client organization informed, and not necessarily for evaluation and approval purposes. When using this mode of specifications, the risk of performance and applicability rest solely and directly with the performing organization. The client is simply responsible for an accurate recitation of the business and strategic objectives for the project. (Figure 2-16)

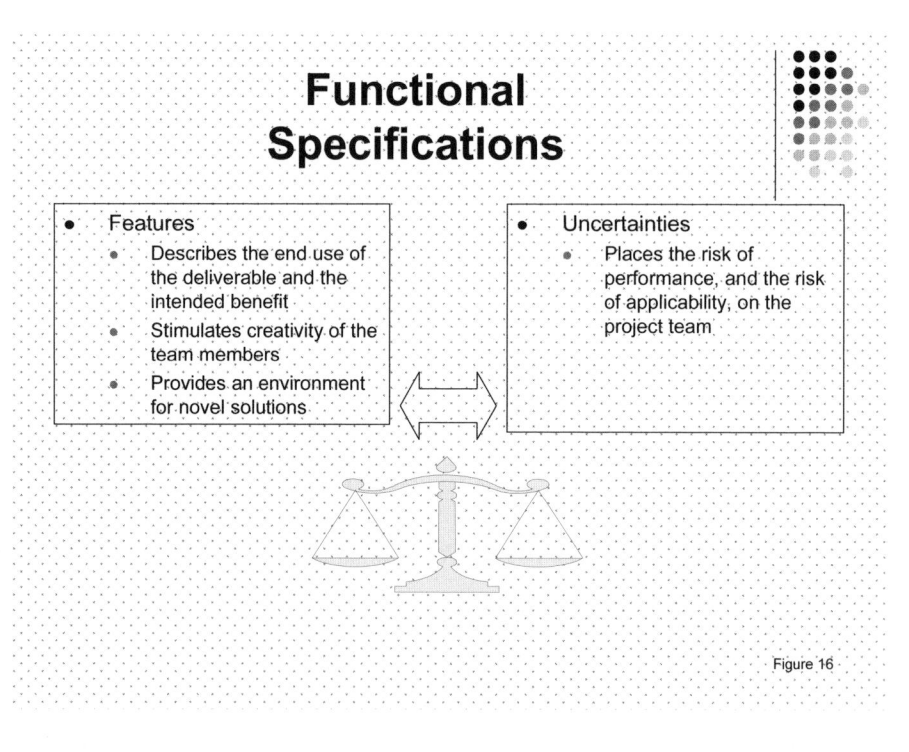

Functional Specifications

- Features
  - Describes the end use of the deliverable and the intended benefit
  - Stimulates creativity of the team members
  - Provides an environment for novel solutions

- Uncertainties
  - Places the risk of performance, and the risk of applicability, on the project team

Figure 16

The role of the specifications documents is minimal in cost-plus-fee contracts, and therefore there is no need to fully develop them during the proposal phase. Typically, the contractor organization will be paid based on how much time and effort is spent, rather than what is produced. In most cases, a cost-plus-fee contractor organization is chosen on the basis of perceived capability and potential reliability, and not necessarily on the basis of a promised total cost or delivery date.

On the other hand, the role of specifications is pivotal in lump-sum contracts, because the specifications will form the basis for the estimate of the real cost of the project, the bid, and the eventual contract price. Midstream modification of the details of a lump-sum contract is difficult, time consuming, and potentially explosive for both parties of the contract. Therefore, lump-sum contracts should be pursued only if the specifications are exceptionally accurate, and if the probability of changes in the specifications is extraordinarily low.

When reviewing specifications, the proposal team must make every effort to understand all of the client's strategic missions, and the underlying rationale for having specified the various facets of the deliverable in that particular fashion. Then, the proposal team must make every effort to meet all the basic strategic missions of the client in a cost effective manner, even if the specifications are ambiguous, self-contradictory, or incomplete.

Ideally, when a set of specifications is presented to the proposal team of the contractor organization, it should contain no flaws or omissions in the statements of scope, specifications, or desired procedures. If that turns out not to be the case, the proposal team should ethically and logically respond by asking questions when there is ambiguity, by listing assumptions when the specifications are incomplete, by taking exceptions when a vision is flawed or unattainable, and by making suggestions when the specifications need improvements.

Such responses would serve the best interests of the client organization, while serving the best long-term interests of the contractor organization. Therefore, under normal circumstances, this philosophy of securitizing the specifications should be the guiding light for all projects/contracts, based on the premise that it fosters a better client-contractor partnership and an environment of trust.

However, there can be instances where taking an active role in the interpretation of the proposal might not serve the short-term interests of the contractor organization. Although the implementation of such a congenial and trusting environment is possible, it is usually approached with some reluctance due to the fact that the obligations, loyalties, and the reward system, for the contractor personnel and client personnel, as delineated by the contract, are different and possibly in conflict with each other.

This philosophy might not be practiced fully and widely in contracting activities because it might subtly and negatively impact the contracting strategy of the performing organization, bidding outcome of this project, and award circumstances of this contract. Therefore, it is traditional that contractors' responses are more in line with compliant responses rather than the seemingly confrontational responses. In some cases, the client organizations reinforce the contractor's passive behavior by rewarding those who exhibit non-feedback, and by punishing those who provide feedback that is not entirely complimentary.

Thus, partly prompted by competitive contracting strategy, and partly in an effort to portray a tendency for being accommodating, prospective lump-sum contractors often offer to comply with all the conditions that are set forth in the contract specifications even if the contractor organization might suspect that the client organization's specifications are flawed. The reinforcing element for this behavior is that the client organizations often regard such conformist behavior in a positive light.

If there are changes to the project specifications during the life of the project, these changes would be grounds for re-negotiating the contract, usually to a higher price. It is not known how many contractors could have predicted the nature and extent of the specification changes of a contract, and chose not to confront the client regarding the quality of the specifications during the proposal phase. Coincidentally, it is commonly believed that contractors of lump-sum contracts tend to prosper when there are a lot of reimbursable change orders during the life of the contract.

2.3 Estimating the Real Cost of the Project

The pricing of the contract begins with a reasonably definitive estimate of the real cost of the project to the performing organization. The estimate of the real cost of the project is simply nothing more than a prediction (albeit an educated prediction) of the total cost of providing people, materials, and equipment for the project. Admittedly, the estimate will be rough during the early steps, partly due to insufficient time for a comprehensive estimate, and partly due to the unavailability of detailed deliverable information. Therefore, it is logical to expect that the estimate of the real values of the project cost and duration should be continually refined and fine-tuned as more information becomes available. Notwithstanding this inevitable variability, the lump-sum contractors are expected to propose a fixed price, and a definitive date, for the delivery of the project.

There are two basic techniques in developing project estimates: direct-indirect, and fixed-variable. The former technique is appropriate for complex projects that have many novel components or many unusual activities, and therefore the estimate might need frequent refinement. The latter is appropriate for making quick estimates of projects, particularly if they do not involve a lot of very complex or little-known components.

The direct-indirect cost estimating technique derives the estimate from calculating the direct costs and indirect costs of conducting the project. Direct costs are those costs that are directly attributable to the project, such as salary of personnel, travel, and cost of buying or renting equipment for the explicit use of the project. One popular way of testing the appropriateness of listing costs of people and equipment as direct costs is to check to see if the listed people and equipment actually came in physical or metaphysical contact with the project deliverable. If personnel or equipment are shared between projects, only a portion of the salary and purchase cost should be included, to the extent that the human/equipment resources were used for the activities of a particular project, and for the duration that they came in contact with the deliverable.

Indirect costs include the costs of infrastructure elements that are necessary for the smooth operation of the project, again to the extent that the resources are indirectly associated with the project. Generally speaking, the infrastructure will contain the costs of providing people resources, and physical resources in support of the core activities of the project. Thus, indirect costs will include portions of the salary of supervisory personnel, who in some way support the project, as well as portions of salaries of the administrative support personnel. Other indirect items are portions of the cost of phone system, faxes, computers, rent, insurance, taxes, and utilities. The cost of items such as sick leave, vacation, training, social security contributions, healthcare, and retirement benefit for the employees, are sometimes listed under direct costs, sometimes under indirect costs, and sometimes under a separate category which is usually titled employee benefits.

Another category of cost that is included in proposals and contracts, as part of the total cost of the project, is overhead. Overhead items are those that do not impact the project even indirectly, but are necessary for the financial and technical health of the performing organization, such as the salaries of the upper executives, cost of unsuccessful proposals, and general upkeep of the organizational headquarters.

Typically, the overhead is not listed as part of the real cost of the projects. However, since sometimes there is an overlap between the definition of indirect and overhead items, often there is a debate between the client organization and the contractor organization as to what items should be included in each category, and how much should be the amount of the items in each category. This debate might become more complicated if the client organization highlights the usual overlap between overhead and profit as a prelude to negotiate the amount of profit. Probably the most straightforward approach to this issue would be to list direct costs and indirect costs in such a way that they can easily be related to the cost of implementing components of the deliverable. Thus, these items become an integral part of the estimate of the real cost of the project, and therefore not easily subject to negotiations or alterations during the contract award phase. (Figure 2- 17)

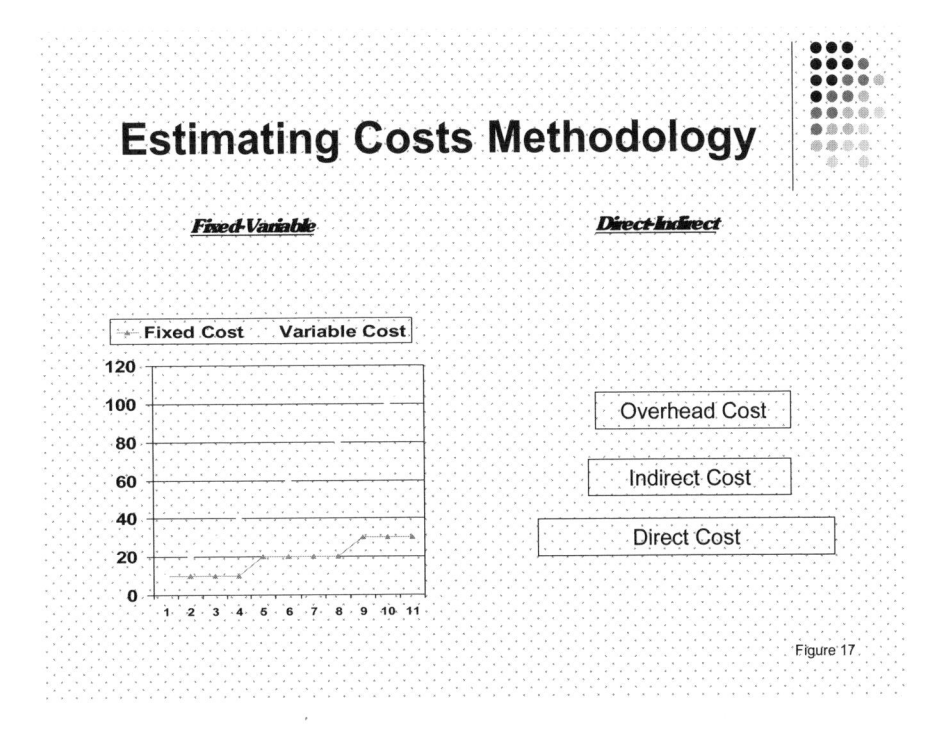

Estimating Costs Methodology

Fixed-Variable

- Fixed Cost
- Variable Cost

Direct-Indirect

- Overhead Cost
- Indirect Cost
- Direct Cost

Figure 17.

The fixed-variable cost technique uses the fixed and variable costs of the total effort in developing the estimate. The fixed and variable concept is most appropriate to the service-oriented contracts, although sometimes it is used to develop an initial estimate of a deliverable-based contract during the early phases of the project. It involves assigning units of service or equipment that would constitute cost-incurring items of the project, which are called variable cost. Examples of variable cost elements are four people, three computers, and 100 feet of fiber optic cable. In this technique, the amount and cost of infrastructure is assumed to be fixed for each block of variable cost items; for example, the project would need one supervisor and two support technicians for any task employing, say, a block of one to four specialists. Thus, if there are seven specialists working on a specific task of the project, the fixed cost would be two supervisors and four support technicians. The fixed cost would be the same for variable efforts of five to eight specialists. The values that are used as the unit price for the fixed costs and variable costs include (probably in an embedded and implicit fashion) the direct, indirect, and overhead, costs of the organization in providing those resources for the project.

After the estimate of the real cost of the project is prepared, an internal budget in line with the estimate should be established for the project. In many ways, the upper management of the organization would become the internal client for the project with the internal budget; even if the project is intended to become an externally-funded project. If the initial project estimate is not exceptionally accurate, the initial internal budget will also carry the same level of accuracy.

In some organizations, the internal budget might be not in monetary terms, but rather in terms of units of labor, equipment, and materials. This technique streamlines the bookkeeping significantly, because there is a direct connection between time of personnel and cost of personnel. However, one important facet of this kind of project budgeting, which is often overlooked, is that when the project manager, who has been assigned, say, three specialists for the execution of the project, makes a request for a two week extension of time, the manager is implicitly requesting for a proportional increase in budget; in addition to requesting for an increase in project duration, of course.

Depending on the circumstances, sometimes the estimate of the real cost, and the resulting internal budget, of the project might not include overhead costs, possibly not even indirect costs. Lastly, although in the case of an internally-funded project there is no mention of profit, in the case of an externally-funded project a significant importance is placed on the issue; to the point that sometimes profit is the major driving force during the proposal preparation steps and during the project performance steps.

2.4 The Bid or the Price of the Contract

A bid and an estimate are two entirely different things, although sometimes clients and contractors use these two terms interchangeably. The estimate is the prediction of the real cost of the project to the performing organization. The bid value, or the price of the contract, which is what the client organization will commit to pay for the contract, will include not only an estimate of the real cost of the project, but also the indirect costs, the overhead costs, and the all-important profit. Thus, the bid value represents a deliberate business proposition that compiles all of those elements.

An estimate is a listing, albeit sometimes not exceptionally accurate, of the forecasted real costs that will be incurred by the performing organization in delivering a project. Naturally, there is always a certain amount of tolerance that is assigned to a forecast. The inaccuracy of the forecast is due to the inaccuracies in determining the amounts of project resources. Notwithstanding, the performing organization must always have specific information on the unit cost of materials and equipment, on the salary of personnel, and on a realistic characterization of the overhead structure of the contractor's organization.

It is an important point that the client organization usually does not see, nor need not be aware of, the inaccurate and dynamically changing forecast of the real cost of the project, primarily because although the estimate of the project is an uncertain value, the price of the (lump-sum) contract is finite and fixed. Further, the bid, or contract price, may not necessarily include details of the various components of the forecasted cost estimate that have formed the basis for the bid. Additionally, these figures might not be necessarily actual or realistic, even if the bid does include details of cost components such as direct costs of labor, materials, and equipment, indirect costs, overhead, contingency, and the all-important return on investment. The amounts included in a bid simply represent the amounts that the contractor is planning to charge for the items of the contract. In some instances, the bid computation of cost values for the deliverable components are values that are developed specifically for the purposes of that specific bid.

The transition from an estimate to a bid is accomplished by adding the overhead and profit amounts to the real cost of the project. This transition is a strategic decision which is based on the probability of occurrence of unexpected events, desirable or undesirable, and based on the bidder's motivation to acquire that particular contract. It must be reiterated that the relationship between the internal budget and the real cost of the project is an operational reality, whereas the relationship between the real cost of the project and the contract price is predicated by a business decision.

When the project estimate is prepared, an internal budget in line with the estimate of the real cost is established for the project. The internal project budget will sponsor the actual burden of the project to the organization. On the other hand, the resulting bid price, that is quoted to the client organization, is not derived linearly from the project estimate. The amount of the proposal bid will be determined by adding indirect costs, overhead, and profit, to the real cost of the project. Then, this total is modified to account for general market conditions, and to account for the motivation of the contractor for obtaining this contract. Depending on the market and business circumstances, the profit margin that the upper management of the performing organization will add to the real cost of the project might vary from zero to a high double digit value. There are rare cases where the upper management of a performing organization has chosen, for business reasons, to charge the client less than the real cost of the project.

One view of the bid development process is to regard the internal budget of the project as having a direct relationship to the real cost of the project, while regarding the price of the contract as having an indirect relationship with the real cost of the project. The direct and indirect descriptors are appropriate because, as the project expends the organizational resources during the execution phase, the performing organization will absorb the real cost of those resources independent of the value of the external budget. The bid price of the externally-funded project reflects the collective combination of the real cost, indirect cost, overhead, and profit; as tempered by general market conditions and the motivation of the contractor for obtaining this contract.

There might be cases where the actual cost of people hours, equipment hours, and materials, that are spent on a project exceed the contractor's estimate. In these cases, the contractor might have to absorb the incremental cost without modifying the contract price. However, since this increase in real cost will diminish the project's profit, all performing organizations are hopeful that the increases in the real cost of the project can somehow be passed along to the client organizations. (Figure 2- 18)

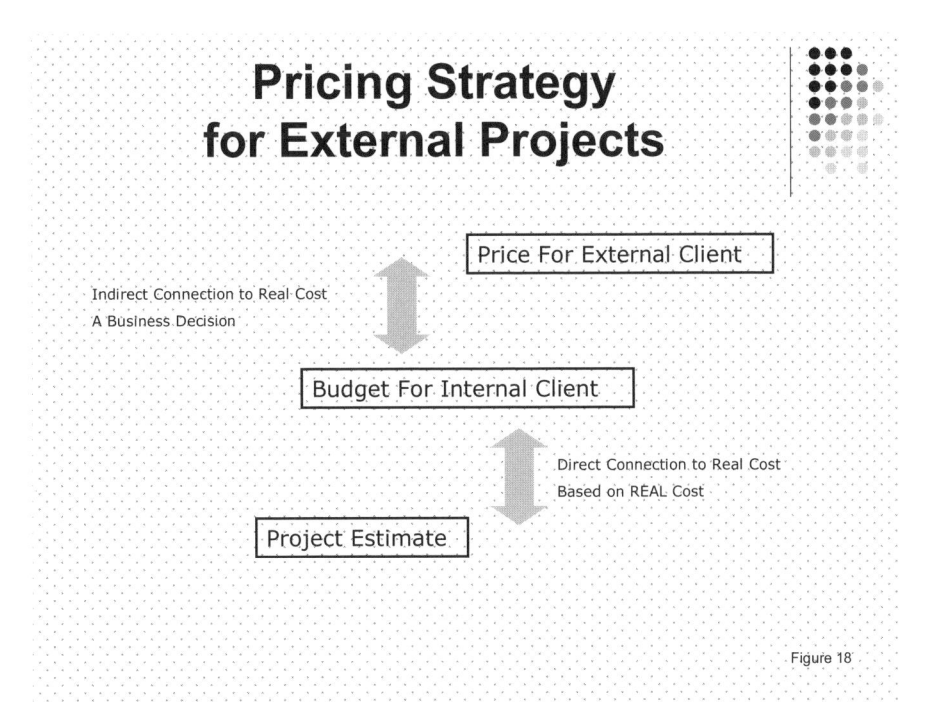

Pricing Strategy for External Projects

Price For External Client
— Indirect Connection to Real Cost
— A Business Decision

Budget For Internal Client
— Direct Connection to Real Cost
— Based on REAL Cost

Project Estimate

Figure 18

Generally, the profit margin of a contract must be in concert with the number of bidders for the same job, primarily because the prospective contractors, in an effort to be the lowest bidder, will reduce the overall profit of the proposal to its lowest possible value. When there are a lot of bidders for the same project, the expected profit margin is very low, while for projects that there are very few bidders, the profit margin can increase accordingly (DeNeufville, Hani, Gates). Experience has shown that a low profit margin will increase the chances of being the successful bidder, although bidding a project below the realistic cost does not necessarily guarantee wining the contract. On the other hand, an extraordinarily high profit margin might reduce the chances of being the successful bidder, although bidding a job with a reasonably high profit margin does not necessarily eliminate all chances of wining the contract. It goes without saying that the most desirable situation for a contractor is one where there are very few bidders for the contract. (Figure 2- 19)

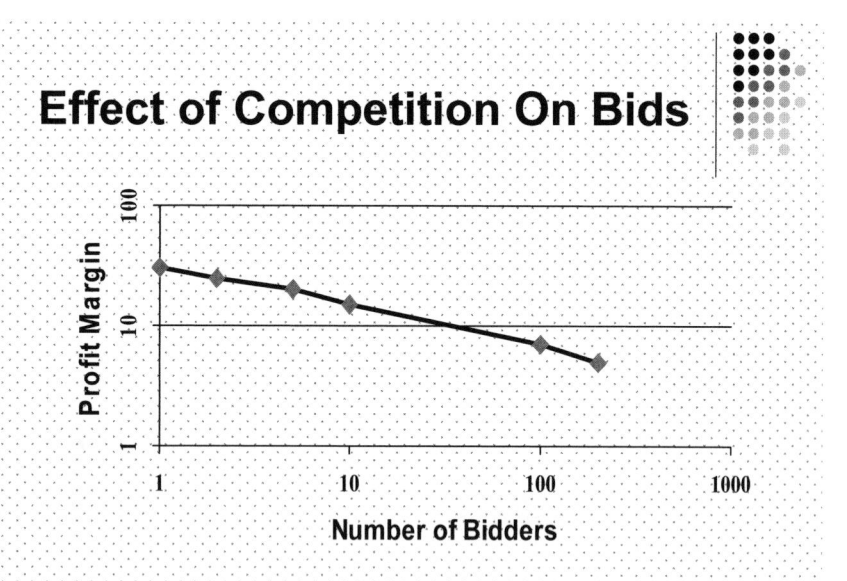

Effect of Competition On Bids

Figure 19

Chapter Summary Preparing a responsive and compelling proposal is the key to winning a contract. A formalized proposal development process will provide consistency in crafting winning proposals. A nominal amount of project planning effort is necessary for developing a responsive price proposal for the prospective project, even in cases where the available project information might not be comprehensive. The specifications of the intended deliverable or service, the conceptual planning performed during the proposal preparation, and the desired profit margin, form the basis for the bid value of the proposal.

3. Contract Phase

The formal definition of a contact is that it is an official and legally-binding record of the understanding between the parties, and that all of the elements of this understanding are enforceable by law. The formal definition further stipulates that the contract should include the method and amount of compensation for the parties. Lastly, a contract must clearly contain an offer by one party, and a formal acceptance of the same by the other party.

A contract for a project obligates the performing organization to a set of specific performance targets, and in turn it obligates the client organization to the payments for these performance targets, sometimes through intricate formulas. The contract will establish clear standards of performance, procedures for reporting, acceptance standards, and dispute resolution guidelines. Additionally, the contract must set procedures, guidelines, and avenues for changing the contract for mutual benefit, during the intermediate reviews of the project, and at the occasions for midstream contract modifications. Further, the contract usually spells out consequences of non-conformance on the part of either party. Finally, a good contract would predict the occurrence of, and will have remedies for, the vast majority of events that one might encounter during the life of the project.

The practical advantages of having a contract are that the contract documents provide specific articulation of the substance, nature, and limitations of the mutual understandings among the parties. By having to document these understandings, the parties will usually be prompted to clarify those understandings, and this exercise will help to avoid any future divergence of objectives. The contract, or rather its precursor which is a request for proposal, becomes the framework for the project that will be implemented by the performing organization. Therefore, within the context of project management, a contract is casually defined as an instrument by which the services, equipment, and material are obtained for the furtherance of the objectives of the client organization. Sometimes, the project client might be the project manager of a larger project within the client organization.

Contracts for prospective projects are usually voluminous compilation of many documents, to the point that often they are overwhelming and intimidating to the uninitiated. These documents can be grouped into two major components: administrative and technical. The technical component of the contract contains specifications for the deliverable, performance targets for the deliverable, or standards of performance for the service portion of the contract. By comparison, the administrative component of the contract includes terms and conditions of payments, reporting guidelines, and management requirements. Contract conditions enumerate issues such as contractor warrantees, remedies for defective work, inspections, change orders, and final acceptance. Reporting guidelines and review meeting processes will outline the frequency of review, means of reporting the progress, and the details of review meetings. Management requirements will enumerate the standards for direct supervision and indirect management of the project team. Of these two components, the administrative component contains complex legal phrasing and language, far more than the technical component.

The administrative component of the contract normally embodies the following two sections: general conditions that apply to most contracts of the client organization, and special conditions that apply specifically to this project. The primary rationale for having a set of general conditions is that, since it does not change often, it obviates the need for the client personnel to draft a new one for every project, and the need for the contractor personnel to study it carefully for each new project. (Figure 3-1)

Contract Documents

- **Envisions all physical and Administrative possibilities; and outlines remedies**
  - General terms and conditions of the client organization
  - Special terms and conditions of this project
  - Reporting guidelines
  - Status review meeting processes
  - Management requirements
- **Presents the Technical data for this job**
  - Statement of work
  - Specifications of the deliverable
    - Narrative descriptions
    - Graphic drawings
    - Tabular data for quantitative attributes

Figure 1

It is very difficult, if not virtually impossible, to produce complete and flawless specifications, as evidenced by the revisions that are issued for many contract specifications documents even as early as during the proposal and bidding stages, and generally during the life of any project. These changes include clarifications of, and modifications to, the project's attributes such as the scope, quality, expected cost, and the desired duration.

As the project progresses into its latter life-cycle phases, the changes to the project would contain more substantive changes and therefore they would impact the WBS, the schedule network, and other detailed planning documents of the project. Additionally, if these baseline modifications are significant enough to impact the contract that governs the project, then the updated planning values would become the basis for a modified contract. Ironically, although by definition the deliverable of a lump-sum project is fully specified before the issuance of the request for proposal, it is possible that a scope change might occur even during the life cycle of a lump-sum project.

In some cases, the project teams from the client organization and the performing organization collectively develop project specifications. Although this collaborative mode of operation is a very useful policy, it has the risk of blending project specifications with project implementation details. This practice also blurs the line between the goals of the project team of the client organization, and the mission of the project team of the performing organization. Further, with an overlap between client-generated material and contractor-generated material, it would then be very difficult to analyze and evaluate the causes of cost and duration over-runs during the execution phase of the project. Accordingly, it will be equally difficult to properly administer and approve the change-orders to the contract, particularly in lump-sum contracts.

Although there is an almost endless list of different types of contracts, contracts can be grouped into three major categories: lump-sum, cost-plus, and unit-price. A lump-sum contract, also known as a fixed-price contract, is one under which the performing organization will receive a specific amount of money from the client

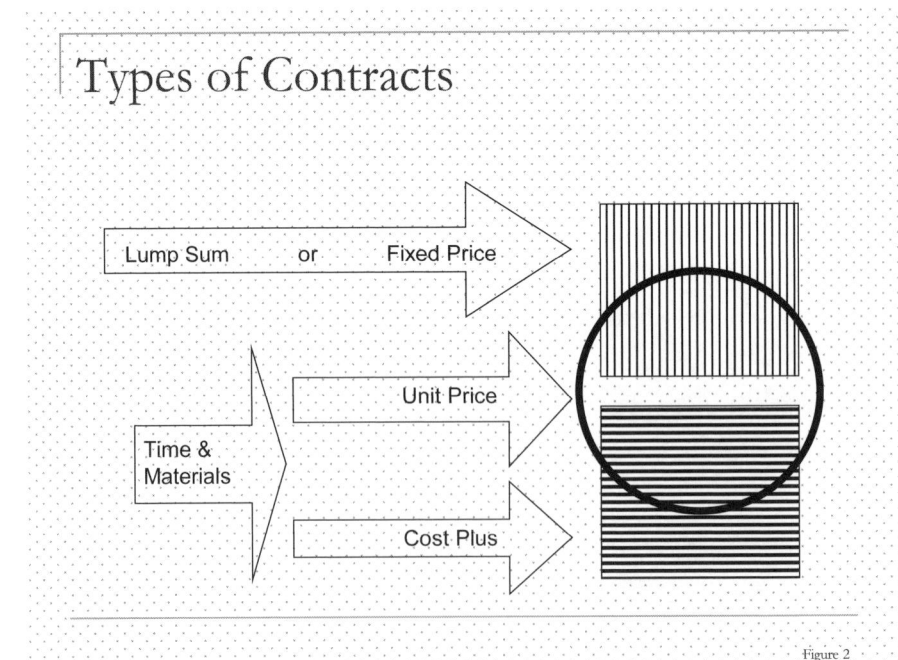

Types of Contracts

Lump Sum or Fixed Price

Unit Price

Time & Materials

Cost Plus

Figure 2

organization for a specific deliverable. A cost-plus contract is one under which the performing organization will be reimbursed from the client organization for its direct costs, plus additional amounts for indirect cost, overhead, and profit (usually expressed in terms of percentages of the actual direct expenditures). A unit-price contract is one where the performing organization is paid for units of service, materials, and equipment, which have been spent toward the mission or the deliverable of the client, on the basis of a pre-agreed unit-price schedule. The term Time-and-Materials (T&M) has been used alternately to refer to the cost-plus mode of contracting, and to the unit-price mode of contracting. (Figure 3- 2)

The texture of the behavior of the parties on both sides of the contract, and the flexibility of their actions, will be vastly different depending on the type of contract that the contracting officer of the client organization has chosen for the forthcoming project. At one end of the spectrum, the employees of the performing organization of a lump-sum contract will be intensely focused on completing the project according the baseline plan and without any variances. At the other end of the spectrum, the employees of the performing organization of a cost-plus contract will be poised to respond to the client organization's instructions, even if these instructions represent major changes of direction. Performing organizations and client organizations are keenly aware of the fact that each of these three major categories of contracts has its own suite of advantages and disadvantages, in terms of behavior, in terms of oversight, and in terms of cash flow and profit.

A lump-sum contract requires that a detailed set of specifications of the deliverable; typically these specifications will be prepared by the client organization and submitted to the performing organization during the bidding process. This category of contract could minimize financial uncertainty, and thus under some circumstances, it could be considered safe for the performing organization. It is an important point that, regardless of whether the financial risk is transferred to the contractor organization, the risk of performance stays with the client organization, because if the contracted project is not successful, the strategic objective that created the project will suffer, independent of the payments toward that contract.

The disadvantages of this category of contract are that it requires an almost flawless set of specifications for proposal preparation and bidding; and that, by extension, the contract modifications could become potentially explosive if the scope is changed during the life of the contract. There is a contracting myth/legend that, in a lump-sum contract environment, contractors usually make a nominal profit if the specifications stay unchanged, and that they are in an enviable position to make handsome profits when and if the specifications change midstream. (Figure 3-3)

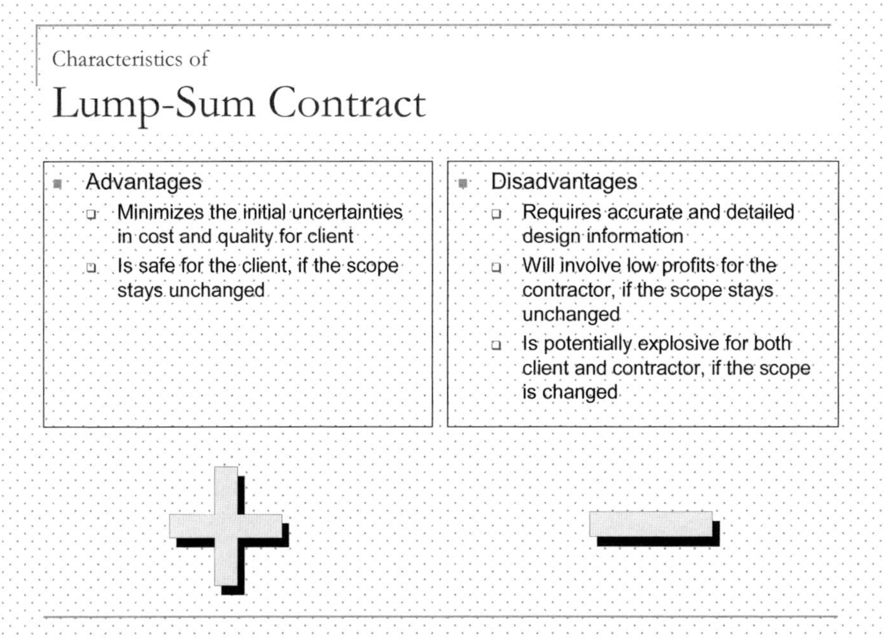

Characteristics of
Lump-Sum Contract

Advantages
- Minimizes the initial uncertainties in cost and quality for client
- Is safe for the client, if the scope stays unchanged

Disadvantages
- Requires accurate and detailed design information
- Will involve low profits for the contractor, if the scope stays unchanged
- Is potentially explosive for both client and contractor, if the scope is changed

Figure 3

A cost-plus contract does not require detailed specifications for proposal preparation and bidding. Instead, the specifications might be developed by the client organization, sometimes in conjunction with the performing organization, in a piecemeal fashion during the execution phase. The payment will include contractually-related expenditures and the additional element of the pre-agreed amount for overhead and profit. The payment to the performing organization is not necessarily based on project progress, but rather on the costs incurred by the performing organization in carrying out the client organization's instructions. From the vantage point of the performing organization, the advantage of this category of a contract is that it protects the cash flow and profit margin of the performing organization. From the vantage point of the client organization, the advantage of a cost-plus contract is that it provides specification flexibilities for the client organization. The primary disadvantage of this category of contract is that it could reduce the motivation of the performing organization for a speedy and efficient project completion. (Figure 3- 4)

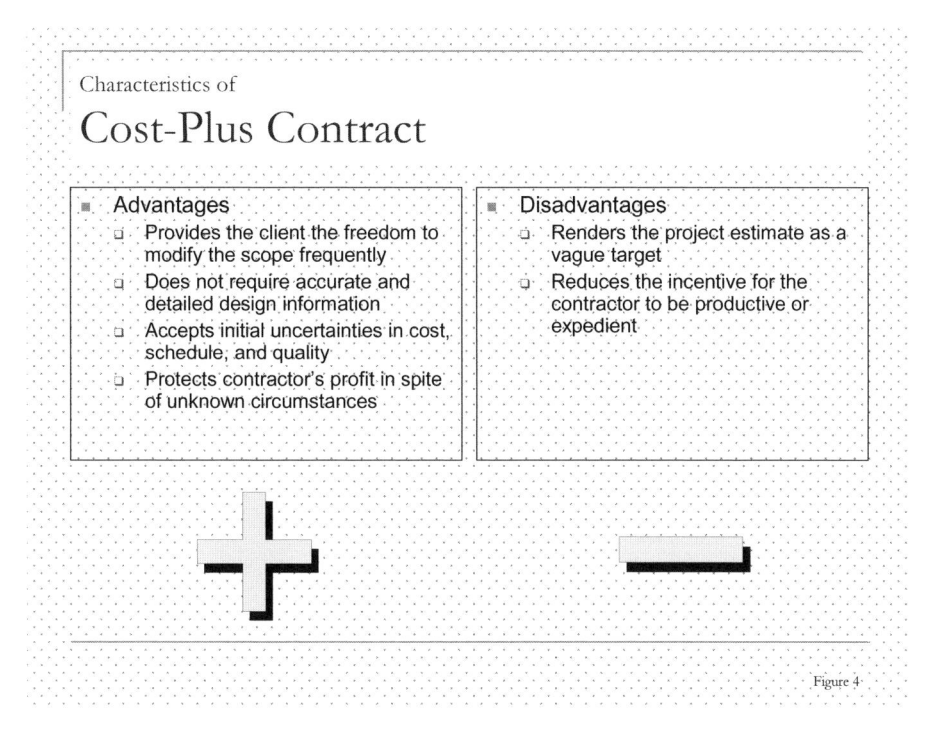

Characteristics of
Cost-Plus Contract

- **Advantages**
  - Provides the client the freedom to modify the scope frequently
  - Does not require accurate and detailed design information
  - Accepts initial uncertainties in cost, schedule, and quality
  - Protects contractor's profit in spite of unknown circumstances

- **Disadvantages**
  - Renders the project estimate as a vague target
  - Reduces the incentive for the contractor to be productive or expedient

Figure 4

The basic contract categories do not fully meet the needs of client organizations and contractor organizations, albeit the list of undesirable attributes might not be the same for the contractor and client organizations. Consequently, to mitigate the adverse effects of these basic categories of contracts, the contract professionals have developed a multitude of contract modifiers. These modifiers are designed to make the management of the issues of the project/contract more straightforward for both parties. These modifiers are usually described with a shorthand notation, such as guaranteed maximum, cost sharing, profit sharing, bonus, and award. In a way, the shorthand notation refers to the general tone of the modifier. Ultimately, the modifications to the basic contract categories are accomplished through the wording of the various detailed clauses within the contract.

Typically, a guaranteed maximum modifier is used with cost-plus-fee contracts to obligate the contracting organization to an upper cost threshold; although usually this threshold is set conservatively high. Profit-sharing modifier will allow the performing organization of a cost-plus-fee project to collect a portion of the under-run amounts if the final project cost is below the initial estimate. Conversely, with a cost-sharing modifier, the performing organization of a cost-plus-fee project will absorb a portion of the cost over-run. The fee-reduction modifier is intended to reduce the fee rate of the contracting organization if the final actual project cost is higher than the original contract estimate, while a fee-increase modifier is intended to increase the fee rate if the final actual cost is lower than the contract estimate.

Contract Modifiers
For Cost-Plus Or Unit-Cost Contracts

- Guaranteed Maximum

- Over-run Cost Sharing
- Under-run Profit Sharing

- Bonus For Under-run
- Bonus For Early Delivery
- Penalty For Overrun
- Penalty For Late Delivery

- Reduced Fee For Being Late Or Over-the-budget
- No Fee After Estimated Date And Cost

- With Award Fee
- With Economic Price Adjustment
  - General inflation
  - Escalation in cost of selected equipment and material

Figure 5

The bonus, penalty, and award fee, modifiers refer to specific payments that are intended to provide incentive for the contracting organization to be efficient in various facets of project delivery. These amounts are usually pre-fixed, and are not dependent on the amount by which the project target was over-run or under-run. The economic adjustment modifier will allow the performing organization of a lump-sum contract to adjust its contract price if the costs of labor and material are increased beyond a pre-defined threshold during the life of the contract. (Figure 3-5)

In order to draft a contract such that it is acceptable to both parties (at least during the award phase of the contract), there is usually a negotiation phase as part of the award of the contract. Sometimes, even after a proposal has been submitted and accepted, there are negotiations to resolve issues that might have caused changes to the basis of the original contract. The negotiation phase might deal with many aspects of the project including overall price, unit price, and quality guidelines. It could also be focused on the amounts that the performing organization may charge for direct cost, indirect cost, overhead, and (real or perceived) profit.

Each of the two major categories of contract has certain risks associated with it, and the parties implicitly or explicitly accept these risks by engaging in that particular form of contract. However, it would be unrealistic to assume that any type of a contract, even with several modifiers, and an array of legal clauses, will provide an iron-clad guarantee of a risk-free venture for either of the parties of the contract. As the first step in mitigating the contract risk, and operational complications, the contracting officer of the client organization must identify the risk item that is to be mitigated. Then the basic contract category, and the modifiers, that best fit the circumstances, will be used in drafting the detailed clauses of the contract. Notwithstanding the basic category and specific clauses that are used, a workable contract is one where all of the objectives of the client organization have been specified in detail and with clarity, and one that allows the performing organization to earn a reasonable profit. (Figure 3-6)

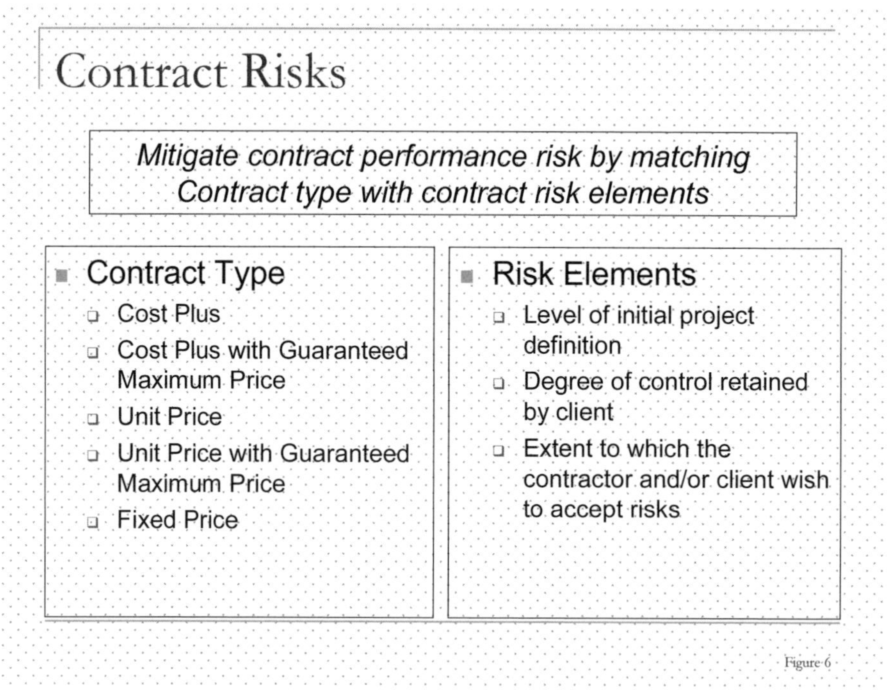

Contract Risks

> Mitigate contract performance risk by matching Contract type with contract risk elements

- **Contract Type**
  - Cost Plus
  - Cost Plus with Guaranteed Maximum Price
  - Unit Price
  - Unit Price with Guaranteed Maximum Price
  - Fixed Price

- **Risk Elements**
  - Level of initial project definition
  - Degree of control retained by client
  - Extent to which the contractor and/or client wish to accept risks

Figure 6

The third category of contract is called a unit-price contract. Under this mode of contract, the performing organization will get paid a specific amount for each unit of work (one hour, one day, etc.), and a specific amount for each unit of material or equipment (one sheet of plywood, one linear foot of fiber optics, one PC, one laptop, etc.). The unit-cost of all of the units of work (people resources and physical resources), which can number in hundreds, will be included in the contract, probably after a relatively lengthy negotiation period. The unit-price contract can be described as a compilation of hundreds of smaller fixed-price contracts with which the performing organization gets paid for the work done on the project in an environment that has traces of cost-plus-fee. Thus, a contract of this category can be regarded as a blend of the cost-plus and lump-sum contracts. That is why unit-price is not considered a major contract category by some contract professionals.

An externally-funded project is the result of a proposal that has passed two separate prioritization processes. One prioritization process is conducted within the performing organization when the performing organization decides to embark on this specific proposal from among all other possible proposals. The second prioritization is conducted within the client organization during the process of selecting the most qualified performing organization for the contract, from among many proposing organizations.

Client organizations usually operate on the notion that selecting the lowest bidder is not necessarily the most logical premise. Therefore, they review all of the pertinent facets of a proposal during their prioritization and selection process. The evaluation of all potential performing organizations, which are sometimes referred to as the prospective contractors, can be assisted by tabulation of the important indices of the data, to the extent that they can be extracted from the various proposals. This form of data tabulation is useful for organizations where the selection process is partially judgment-based and debate-oriented. With the aid of this table, the evaluation team would debate the significance of the individual indices of this table, and the responsiveness of each proposing organization to that index. Then, through discussion and debate, the evaluation team would somehow combine the results of

Simple Contractor Evaluation Matrix

	WBS Package A	WBS Package B	WBS Package C	WBS Package D	Responsive	Previous Experience
Initial Estimate	20,000,000	3,500,000	7,900,000	900,000		
Budget	20,000,000	1,000,000	5,000,000	1,000,000		
Contractor 1	19,900,000	9,900,000	4,900,000	9,900,000	Partly	Some Friction
Contractor 2	24,000,000	700,000	700,000		Mostly	Good Relations
Contractor 3		310,000			Fully	Some Friction
Contractor 4	18,900,000					Late Delivery

Figure 7

all of the elements in order to identify the most appropriate performing organization for this contract. (Figure 3-7)

A relatively more formalized process can be devised for ranking the potential performing organizations for a particular contract. This process would use a model with a WBS-like structure that includes quantified values. The elements of this ranking model could include those relating to the planning details of the proposal at hand, and those relating to the predicted future behavior of the contractor as determined from documented performance of the performing organization in previous contracts. The behavior index refers to the personal attributes such as openness, responsiveness, and cordiality of the contractor personnel. It is an important point that not only personal behavioral attributes are a significant element of the perceived performance of the contractor, but they can sometimes be linked to the real performance of the contractor.

The indices shown on this illustration have been assumed to be appropriate for this mythical organization. However, the list of indices is fully expected to be different for each organization, in line with that organization's strategic missions. The scoring points for these indices are quantitative indications of the importance of each particular index to the organization, although another organization might assign entirely different points of importance to their indices, even if that organization uses the same suite of indices. Lastly, this illustration is for a lump-sum contract. If the client organization uses a cost-plus contract, then the technical competence and probability of success should also be included in the model.

The total number of possible points that a performing organization can achieve is 100. For this mythical organization, technical capability has a weight of 70 points, while the behavioral attributes have a weight of 30 points. The prospective contractor shown in this example scored 42/70 points for the technical capability, and 18/30 points for the behavioral attributes. Thus, the total score for this prospective performing organization is 60/100. Having this data available for the entire proposal pool, the prioritization of the prospective contractor organizations will be completed by compiling a list of the performing organizations that is ranked by their points as derived from this model. It bears repeating that the absolute values of the total scores calculated for each proposing organizations is not nearly as important as are the relative values calculated for all of the organizations within the bidders pool. (Figure 3-8)

Contractor Evaluation Indices
Example

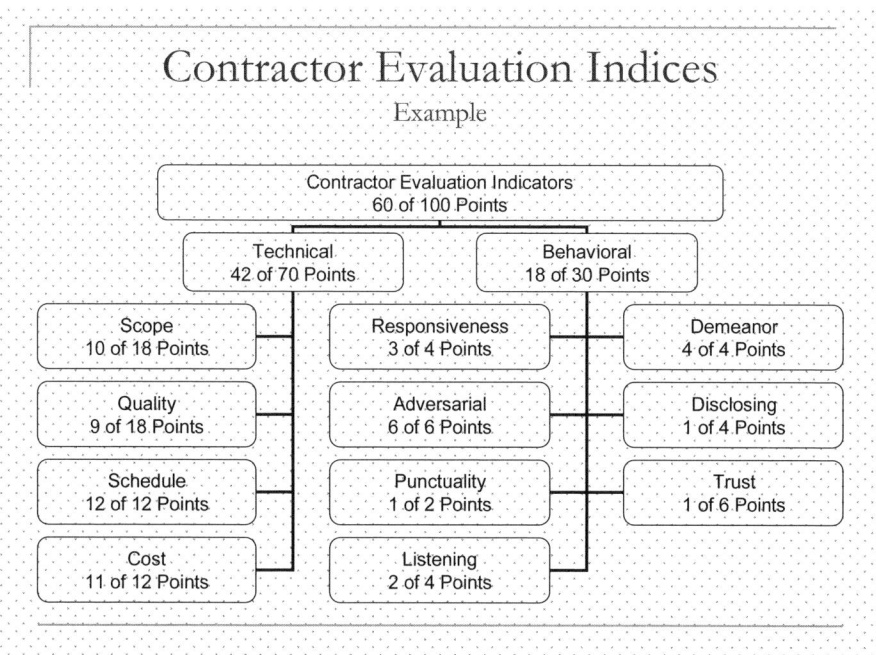

Contractor Evaluation Indicators
60 of 100 Points

- **Technical** — 42 of 70 Points
  - Scope — 10 of 18 Points
  - Quality — 9 of 18 Points
  - Schedule — 12 of 12 Points
  - Cost — 11 of 12 Points
- **Behavioral** — 18 of 30 Points
  - Responsiveness — 3 of 4 Points
  - Adversarial — 6 of 6 Points
  - Punctuality — 1 of 2 Points
  - Listening — 2 of 4 Points
  - Demeanor — 4 of 4 Points
  - Disclosing — 1 of 4 Points
  - Trust — 1 of 6 Points

Figure 8

Chapter Summary A contract formalizes the duties of the performing organization, and the responsibilities of the client organization, with respect to the project. The contract obligates the performing organization to certain elements of service or delivery, and the client organization to specific payments. There are three types of contracts: Lump-Sum, Cost-Plus, and Unit-Price. None of these contract categories is risk-free for the client or for the performing organization. Therefore a large array of contract modifiers has been developed whose functions are to clarify the agreement represented by the contract, to minimize the project performance risk, and to mitigate the financial risk of the project for both parties.

4. Performance and Monitoring Phase

Once a mutually agreeable set of terms have been negotiated and recorded, the contract is signed by both parties. At that point, the proposing organization is regarded as having been awarded the contract, and the proposing organization will become the performing organization. Then, the performing organization will mobilize its resources and execute the project in accordance with the contract. From this point forward, the project manager will focus on delivering the ultimate product of the project using the accepted project management tools and procedures, and with careful and constant attention to the contract clauses.

If a detailed set of project plans was not prepared as part of the proposal step, then the project execution will be preceded by a comprehensive planning effort. The plans that will be developed at this stage will have details of elemental resource requirement, elemental cost, and the implementation schedule, of the project deliverable. The planning process will also produce guidelines for handling quality of the deliverable, for responding to risk events, and for dealing with the inevitable changes to the project plan.

Project planning is the art and science of predicting the resource expenditures, total cost, and total duration of a project. This prediction will be an educated prediction if it is conducted on the basis of the archived historical information, personal expertise, institutional memory, organizational knowledge, and project scope statement. Other necessary information for a comprehensive and accurate set of plans includes details of the project specifications, including its scope statement, targeted quality, and desired delivery date.

Enlightened project managers believe that there are significant time-savings to be achieved by starting the project with a detailed planning phase. The notion is that the cost and effort of an initially detailed planning will be paid back many times during the execution and change management phases. A carefully planned project will avoid the extensive and painful efforts in trying to remedy cost over-runs, schedule over-runs, and delivery defects. There is an inverse relationship between planning effort and modification effort. Projects that were initiated after a careful and detailed planning, and by extension have formalized bases for monitoring and modification, would require less effort during the modification phase of the project.

By contrast, projects that were started with minimal planning, and with casually evolving plans, tend to be plagued with extensive and expensive ad-hoc remedial efforts in order to deal with the unexpected changes that might occur during project modification phase. Often, the remedial project plans are not fully successful in getting the project back on track. (Figure 4- 1)

Extent of Plan Modifications

There is an inverse relationship between the quality of the original project plans and the amount and intensity of changes during the performance phase

Extent of plans during the initiation/planning phase

Extent of modifications during the performance phase

Plan → Modify the Plan →

Detailed Plan → Modify →

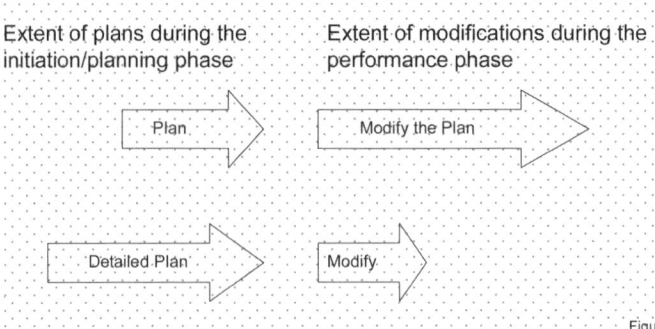

Figure 1

Therefore, it is essential that the project team conduct a careful early planning in order to set the stage for significantly minimizing the frequency and impact of unexpected events, that would in turn require changes to the project plan. If the project is implemented with careful planning, many of the changes will be anticipated, and the team will institute remedies for them as they begin to materialize. It would be unrealistic to expect good planning to eliminate the occurrence of all of the unexpected events, but it is logical to expect good planning practices to result in a dramatic reduction of the magnitude and impact of project changes that are triggered by unexpected events.

In order to develop a detailed and logical set of estimates for cost and duration of the project, two separate structures need to be created, defined, or modified for the purposes of a project: The Work Breakdown Structure (WBS), and the Resource Breakdown Structure (RBS). The WBS is the well-recognized schema by which all of the constituent elements of the project are identified and categorized. The WBS should be deliverable-based in that all of the elements of the WBS should describe the physical, or metaphysical, items that the client expects to receive once the project is completed. Likewise, the RBS is the schema by which all of the resources that would be necessary for the project will be identified, priced, and categorized. Each of the RBS elements should designate a resource by its function-specific description. Additionally, each resource should have its own unit of measure, and the cost of that unit.

As project details become available, they in turn will trigger enhancements in the WBS, the RBS, the estimate, the schedule, and other planning documents of the project. With the availability of these comprehensive structures, project planning becomes organized and very comprehensive. Then, having a clear set of project plans, project success becomes more achievable and more logical, through accurate reporting, and regular updating.

As the first step toward developing the estimate of the project cost, and of the project duration, the project team will identify the various constituent physical elements, and related activities, that are necessary to meet the project objectives. Based on this information, the project team will estimate the amount of resources, and length of time, that is necessary for each of the constituent elements of the project. For each constituent element, the estimate of the amount of resources will be converted to the estimate of cost using the unit price of that particular resource. The project team will then develop the estimate of the cost of the total project by summing the estimates of the cost of the resources for all of the constituent elements of the project; this process is sometimes called rolling-up. This process is aptly called Bottom-Up Estimating. The Bottom-Up estimate technique is the preferred choice because it is far more accurate and far more sophisticated than other estimating methods, even though admittedly creating the WBS and RBS structures would require a nominal amount of time and effort at the beginning of the project. (Figure 4-2)

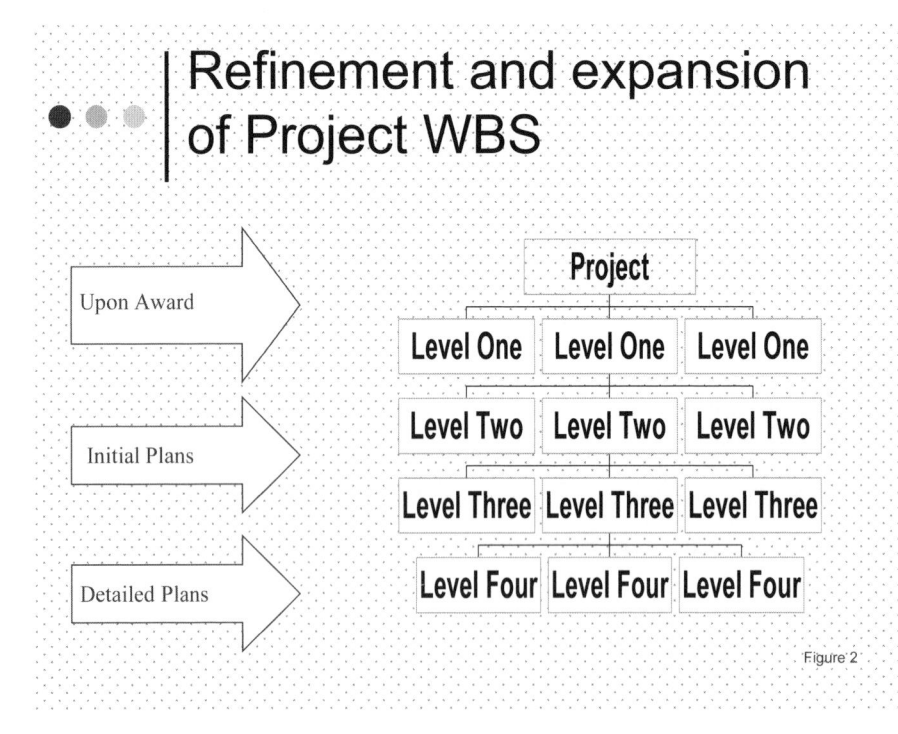

Refinement and expansion of Project WBS

Upon Award

Initial Plans

Detailed Plans

Project
- Level One | Level One | Level One
- Level Two | Level Two | Level Two
- Level Three | Level Three | Level Three
- Level Four | Level Four | Level Four

Figure 2

Realities are that when the project is conceived, the first estimates of the cost and duration are inaccurate because very little information is available about the expected deliverables, about the project team, and about the project environment. Thus, it is highly advisable that the project plans be updated regularly and frequently, even if there are no changes in scope. As the project evolves in its phases of development, and as more information becomes available, the estimates can be, and must be, fine-tuned to a higher level of accuracy. Planning documents might also include increasing details about the procedures that will be used in implementing the project. Lastly, notwithstanding the efforts to continually fine-tune the project plans, additional changes in project cost and duration might become necessary if the client specifications are modified, if the project environment turns out to be different than anticipated, and if the client organization alters its vision for the design philosophy.

There is usually not sufficient time or information available for planning during the proposal phase of proposals, except possibly for the lump-sum category of a contract. The practice of developing detailed estimates is invaluable in lump-sum contracts because it protects the profit margin of the performing organization by predicting the real cost of project more accurately. Conceptually, due to the nature of the process by which projects are initiated, in any category of a contract there is always a good likelihood that there will be changes to the project plans, and the project team must be skillfully prepared to deal with those inevitable changes. Typically, the changes in specifications are more likely to occur in a cost-plus-fee environment, where the contractual difficulty of handling changes is much less pronounced than in a lump-sum environment.

The estimates of the cost, and duration, of the WBS elements, and the estimates for the total project, are initially developed during the early stages of the project. These values will form the baseline budget for measuring the cost/schedule performance of the project during the early stages of the implementation phase. It is fair to say that the cost estimate, and hence the internal budget, is initially very rough and inaccurate; and so is the anticipated delivery date. When establishing the project's internal budget on the basis of the project estimate, one must keep in mind whether the estimate was developed using a rough conceptual estimate technique, or whether the estimate was developed using a detailed bottom-up estimate. If the internal budget were established during the early stages of the project planning, it will carry a high degree of inaccuracy. Accordingly, in a mature and sophisticated organization, the amount of internal budget for the project will continually go through enhancements as the details of the project are developed more clearly.

As for predicting the project duration, during the early stages of the project planning, a total overall estimate of project duration can be obtained using any one of the rough scheduling models available. However, as more details of the project become available, a more definitive, more logical, and more accurate depiction of the project's duration will become possible. The estimates of the duration for each of the project constituent elements are prerequisites to developing a project schedule, particularly if the elemental estimate includes resource intensity and

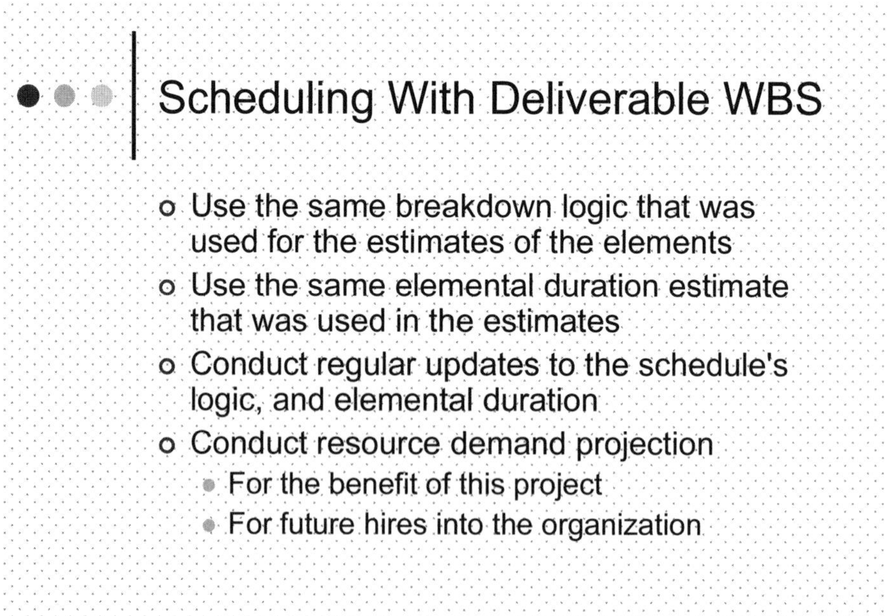

Scheduling With Deliverable WBS

- Use the same breakdown logic that was used for the estimates of the elements
- Use the same elemental duration estimate that was used in the estimates
- Conduct regular updates to the schedule's logic, and elemental duration
- Conduct resource demand projection
  - For the benefit of this project
  - For future hires into the organization

Figure 3

resource duration. There is a hopeful expectation that cost estimating and scheduling processes use the same WBS elements as their foundation.

Whereas the estimating the cost of the project is achieved by a simple rolling up of the costs of corresponding lower level elements, the estimate of the duration of the project is not a simple addition but calculated using the execution sequence of the WBS elements. The execution sequence is usually depicted graphically in a diagram commonly known as schedule network logic diagram. As the details of the project become more accurate, then the duration and delivery date of the project should be updated through calculations that are performed using a network logic diagram that incorporates enhanced sequencing, and enhanced elemental duration estimates. Ideally, the estimate of cost and the estimate of duration should be developed during the same update process. (Figure 4-3)

A detailed elemental WBS structure would have the added utility of facilitating the assignment of the project's constituent elements to individual team members. Thus, the accountability of the team members and the project manager will be clear and unmistakable. It is far more useful to create job titles that are specific to project

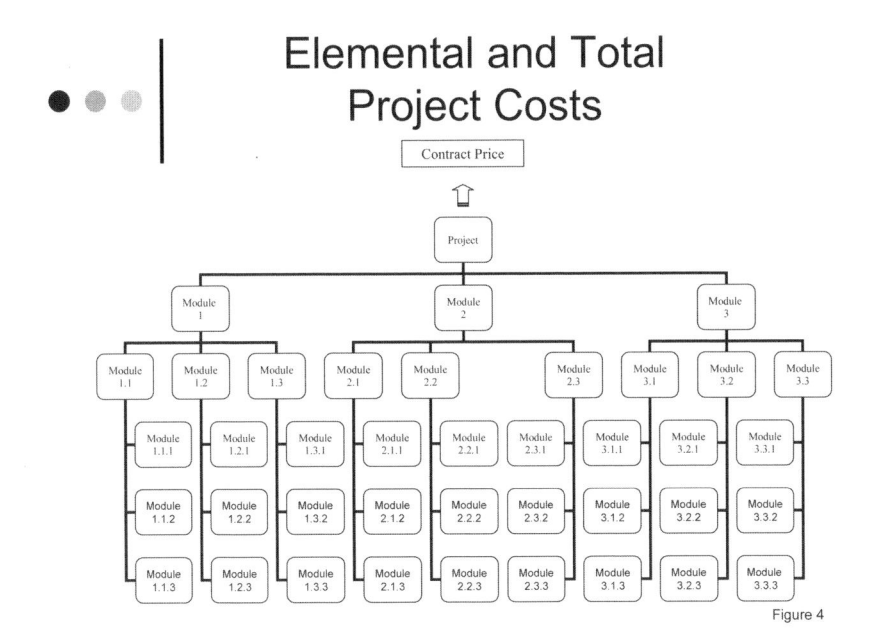

Elemental and Total Project Costs

Figure 4

management, rather than generic organizational titles. If the job titles are function-specific, then the resource planning, cost estimating, and progress reporting of projects becomes simpler and yet more meaningful. Then, by extension, the issue of rewarding the high performing team members becomes very straightforward. (Figure 4-4)

Unsophisticated organizations, who do not engage in detailed planning, often find monitoring and change-management of project difficult and to some extent mysterious. Sadly, their solution almost always is to broaden and expand the monitoring activities, recording tools, and reporting processes,. This line of thinking produces disappointing results primarily because project monitoring needs a clear baseline for the determination of variances, which is precisely the missing ingredient here.

By comparison, sophisticated organizations use fine-tuned planning models and extensive historical data, to develop detailed and accurate estimates. In turn, not only the change management process is conducted on an informed basis and in a

Project Cost Elements

- Real hours
  - Overtime hours
    - Time charged
    - Time not charged
- Real cost
  - For this contract
  - For future models
- Internal budget
- Costs absorbed by the internal client
- External contract price
- Costs reimbursed by the external client

Figure 5

very straightforward fashion, but the monitoring process can provide a wealth of historical information that will be invaluable for future projects.

During the project execution, the following information should be the minimum that is collected for each of the project's constituent elements: real cost, real hours, internal budget, portion absorbed, portion added to the contract price. Thus, once the data is rolled up to the project level, the summarized data for the entire project is highly accurate and pertinent. During the project closeout, the project's historical information will be distilled to provide lessons learned, and to enhance the indices and values of the planning models for future projects. (Figure 4-5)

The progress is normally measured in the areas of cost, schedule, and scope. The baseline data might be the original baseline data, although in most cases it is a modified version of the original baseline as a result of the continuous fine-tuning of the project plans. Provided that there is a formalized progress monitoring system in force, the observed variances in resource expenditure, in cost, and in project duration, will be used to identify trends, which will in turn become the trigger for midstream adjustments to project plans. The reliance on RBS and WBS, will allow the project team to compile meaningful historical data which will be directly applicable to managing the changes in the texture of the current project, while providing useful historical data for facilitating more informed estimating and managing of future projects.

The organizational improvement cycle for the planning processes is such that the accuracy and efficiency of the initial estimate of project cost and duration depends on data collected from previous experiences in similar projects. In turn, a formalized monitoring system will produce a new set of historical data for fine-tuning the cost estimating and schedule development models. Progressively more efficient cost and duration estimating models will benefit the accuracy of the planning, and effectiveness of monitoring, of future projects. In essence, although the progress monitoring system benefits the project at hand significantly, it has far reaching benefits for the future projects, and for organizational project management effectiveness as a whole. (Figure 4-6)

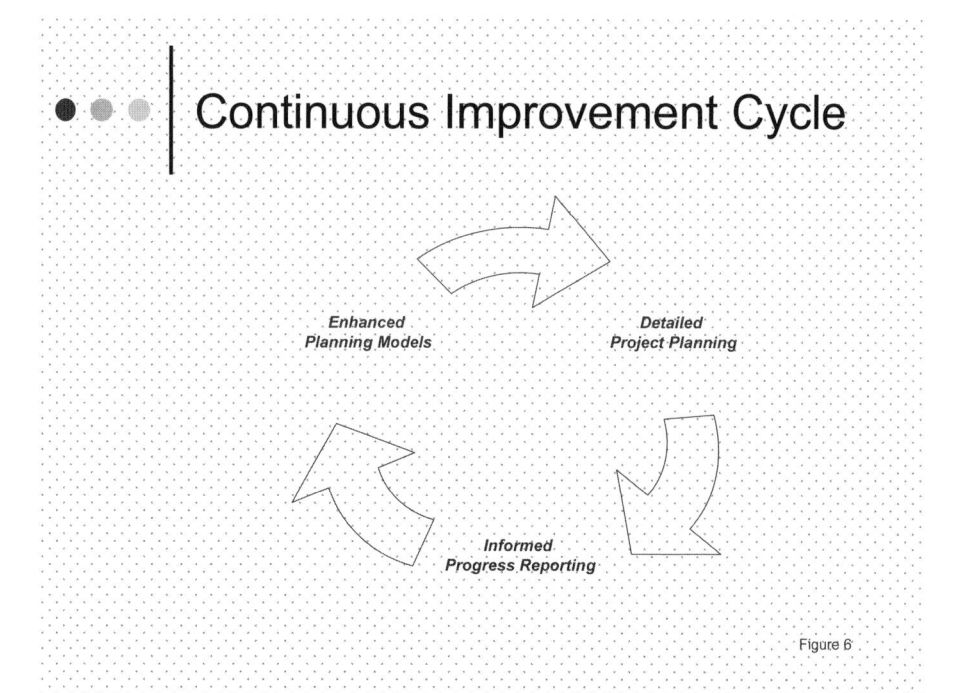

Continuous Improvement Cycle

Enhanced Planning Models

Detailed Project Planning

Informed Progress Reporting

Figure 6

Formalized and extensive monitoring of project performance is essential to the process of keeping the project team, and the client organization, informed of the status of the project deliverable. Data that is collected during the progress monitoring process is crucial in managing the issues and circumstances that will be triggered by the inevitable changes to the project. The purpose of progress monitoring is not to force the project progress, and its associated real costs, to the figures that were pre-defined as part of the plans and budget, but rather it is to report accurate values of actual project performance indices, with hopes of developing remedies for the significant variances.

The function of a progress monitoring system is to keep each project team member informed of the progress of his/her own task, and apprised of the progress in the attainment of the overall objectives by all of the team members. As such, the progress monitoring system should be regarded as nothing other than a valuable aid. It is unfortunate that, in many of the creativity-based projects, the project team might regard progress reporting as cumbersome, intrusive, and a signal that the senior management does not trust the project team. Project managers, who use progress data for pressuring individual task leaders to deliver products faster, often reinforce and perpetuate these sentiments by their very actions. Further, divisional managers, who with a misguided objective of efficiency and improvement, use progress data to micro-manage the project team, provide unwitting affirmation for the team's negative attitude towards progress monitoring tools.

In projects that involve a great deal of creativity and new technology, project team members regard progress monitoring as an affront to creativity. Ironically, a logical progress monitoring system would not impede creativity, but rather would assist the team members in understating the cost/schedule implications of their contributions to the project, thus allowing the project professionals to concentrate on producing superior deliverables. With proper education and indoctrination, the majority of the team members and upper management will hopefully adopt a healthier and more appropriate view of progress monitoring.

The progress monitoring system should be formulated and implemented such that it will not negatively impact the efficiency, creativity, innovation, and morale of the technical personnel of the project team. Rather, it must be a facilitative tool that informs the team members of their individual assignments, reminds them of forthcoming events, and warns them if there are significant variances. Additionally, the progress monitoring system will centrally store the data for forecasting, and for future customization of estimating models.

4.1 Earned Value

In some organizational environments, lapsed time, and accrued cost of labor, are considered indications of progress. Although these indicators are good means to measure the incurred real cost, they do not have a direct relationship with progress, and therefore they can be misleading and highly inaccurate for progress reporting purposes. A more rational set of progress indicators would include measurements of what has been delivered, and indications of the rate of resource expenditures with respect to each deliverable. Examples of progress indicators in construction projects are number of feet of wire pulled, cubic yards of concrete poured, or square feet of carpet installed. Examples of progress indices in systems development projects are number of screens completed, number of lines of code written, or number of machines enabled.

Probably the most well-known formalized technique for monitoring the progress of the project is the determination of the Earned Value. Generally speaking, the earned value is a definitive indication of how much progress has been made in delivering the final project deliverable. Traditionally, the earned value is derived from the four terms that are listed below. The values of these terms must be refreshed often, at least during the evaluation milestones of the project.

- PV, Planned Value
    What was planned to be done
- AC, Actual Cost
    What was spent
- EV, Earned Value
    What was done
- BAC, Budget at Completion
    Amount budgeted for the entire project

Then, the following series of evaluative and predictive ratios will be calculated in order to assess the current state of the project, and to predict the future direction of the project.

- EV-AC=CV Cost Variance
    The amount of cost over-run or under-run
- EV-PV= SV Schedule Variance
    The schedule over-run or under-run in $
- EV/AC=CPI Cost Performance Index
    Normalized cost over-run or under-run
- EV/PV= SPI Schedule Performance Index
    Normalized schedule over/under run
- BAC/CPI=EAC Estimate at Completion
    Updated estimate of total project cost
- BAC-EAC= VAC Variance at Completion
    Amount of over/under run at delivery
- (BAC-PV)/CPI= ETC Estimate to Complete
    Funds needed to complete the project

The concept of earned value is one of most effective perspectives in monitoring the progress of externally-funded fixed-price contracts where the objective is to calculate the amount of payment that is due to the performing organization during the midstream payment occasions. The values that are derived using this concept will precisely determine the portion of the payment that the contractor has earned by calculating the amount of deliverables produced as of the reporting date.

However, to the extent that earned value reflects the magnitude of progress, the earned value can serve as an equally powerful tool in determining the rate of progress of internally-funded projects toward achieving the goals of the project. Therefore, computation of earned value must be integrated into the progress monitoring system of all projects.

For creativity-based tasks, where the deliverable of a single task often defies measurement, and where progress is an illusive and immeasurable concept, guidelines need to be established as to how to ascertain the elemental progress. Depending on the organizational culture, project complexity, and the needs of the project, one of several crediting methods can be applied. In some cases, progress credit can be applied when the task is started and credit can be applied incrementally (say 0%, 30%, 60%, 90% and 100%) as apparent progress is made. Yet, in other organizational environments, one must apply a binary system to signify the progress of the task in question, in that credit is applied only when the completed element of the deliverable is received. Under this system, no credit will be applied for progress if the deliverable has not been received, regardless of how much time and money has been spent on the task.

The rationale for the development and use of these crediting schemas is to provide elemental progress data as accurately as possible with minimal intrusion into the technical facets of a particular creativity-based task. The assigned progress credit percentages do not have to be exceptionally accurate; in fact, due to the nature of many creativity-based projects, normally the accuracy of the assigned credit percentages is somewhat low. Notwithstanding the inaccuracy of this value at the lowest level, once the earned values are rolled up to the project level, the accuracy is acceptable, if there are no overt biases in determining the elemental credits.

Thus, at any point during the life of the project, one can determine the amount of progress, as indicated by the earned value of the project, by summarizing the earned values of lower level elements of the WBS along the WBS structure. Then, on the basis of the results of the earned value exercise, the project team may make an informed determination that the variances are transient and not significant, and that no major changes need to be made. Alternately, the project team might use the progress data as a basis for making adjustments to the work pace. With respect to the cost of remedies, the project team might conclude that it is appropriate to draft a budget request for a modification to the internal budget. The next step would be the delicate decision of whether or not to request a change in contract price from the external client.

Given that current project management practices involve storing a relatively massive amount of data on the project's individual constituent WBS elements, the amount of earned value can be calculated for each of the individual elements with reasonable accuracy. During the latter phases of the project, more accurate predictions of completion cost and duration can be obtained from an updated schedule network, and from an updated bottom-up estimate. Prediction of final cost can be achieved from a roll-up of the updated estimates, and prediction of the final duration can be achieved from the updated network. In turn, the progress in achieving the overall cost and schedule targets, and their final predicted delivery values, can be derived from the detailed elemental data. The calculation of the progress rate indicators, and final delivery values, can be accomplished very conveniently and almost automatically. The progress values, and by extension the earned values, obtained through this schema are far more accurate and traceable than those obtained by the usual three-letter-acronym predictive methods.

The three-letter-acronym schema is a highly enduring and most well-known schema that is used to determine the earned value. This technique was developed primarily for lump-sum contracts, and well before the advent of computers. Therefore, the unit of measure of the primary indices of this technique is dollars, even for the index that is intended to highlight schedule status. Additionally, this technique uses linear extrapolation in predicting future values of project cost and project duration; which is acceptable as a first approximation, but not exceptionally accurate for detailed analysis.

Thus, although there is no question that the concept of earned value is an exceptionally useful concept, the techniques to determine earned value are due for an enhancement. However, since many project and contract personnel relate very comfortably to the traditional calculation schema that uses the familiar acronyms, it is still widely used to report project progress, and to predict the final project cost

Performance Phase

and duration. Therefore, the transition to a more accurate technique for calculating EV might take a significant amount of time.

It bears repeating that, independent of what schema is used to determine the earned value, the calculation of earned value has been found to be an enormously effective tool in measuring progress of contractors in external projects, and the progress of the performing teams of internal projects.

4.2 Client Relations

From a broad perspective, the stakeholders of a project tend to be the same groups of individuals independent of the sources of funds; they are the organizational upper management, the project team, customers, and users. The distinction is that the stakeholders of an internally-funded project all reside in different operational units of the same organization. By contrast, in an externally-funded project, the customers, users, and client, reside in an entirely different organization, which is

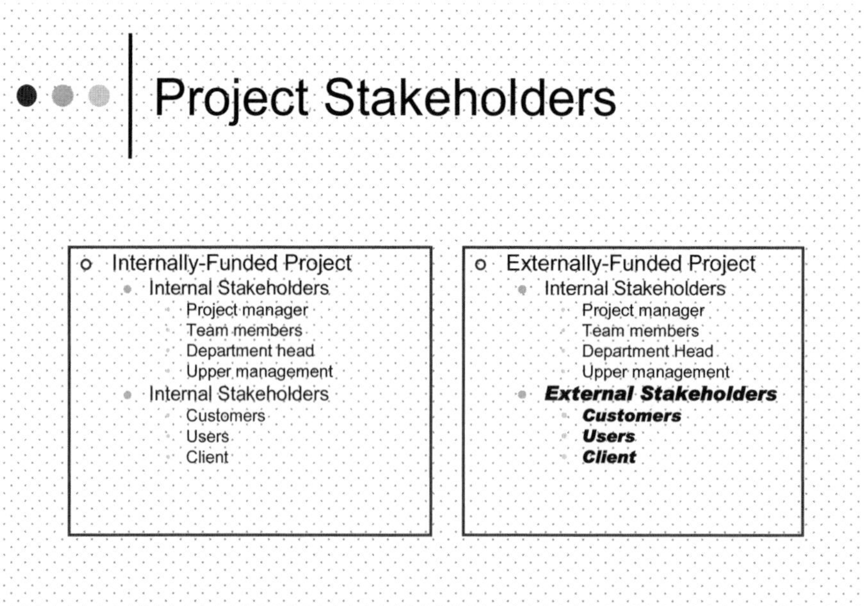

Project Stakeholders

- Internally-Funded Project
  - Internal Stakeholders
    - Project manager
    - Team members
    - Department head
    - Upper management
  - Internal Stakeholders
    - Customers
    - Users
    - Client

- Externally-Funded Project
  - Internal Stakeholders
    - Project manager
    - Team members
    - Department Head
    - Upper management
  - **External Stakeholders**
    - **Customers**
    - **Users**
    - **Client**

Figure 7

separated from the performing organization by virtue of a contract.

The client-contractor line of demarcation is always in the forefront of all of the interactions between the project and the client, regardless of how successfully a partnership spirit has been infused into the environment. The presence of a contract creates an environment of delineated objectives that sometimes precludes a common focus on the project by the client and the contractor. Lastly, the behavior and duties of an organization will be vastly different depending on whether the organization is the client of the contract or the performer of the contract's project, and depending on the characteristics of the prevailing contract. (Figure 4-7)

Independent of whether the project is internally-funded or externally-funded, the project manager would need to continue a dialogue with the client, albeit the communication is far more formalized in the case of an externally-funded project. The importance of client relations is more subtle in internally-funded projects and more explicit in externally-funded projects. When handling client relations issues, the project manager not only will have to attend to issues of the project, but also be mindful of maintaining client goodwill, and the extent to which the performance of this project will set the stage for getting future contracts from the same client.

The realities of the contracting environment are that proposals are often generated or solicited based on previous performance, and directly tied to client relations. Even if the forthcoming opportunity is advertised through a public or semi-public solicitation, the likelihood of winning a future contract is sometimes indirectly tied to the sophistication by which client relations are practiced in the current contract. Thus the client relations issues are in the forefront of the decisions, not only during the proposal and contract award steps, but also during the delivery and acceptance steps, and finally during the chargeback and claims phases.

Each project will have an internal operating budget which is assigned to it by the upper executives of the performing organization. This budget is based on the estimate of the real cost of the project at the beginning of the project, and will be modified, at prescribed points throughout the life of the project, again based on the updated estimate of the real cost of completing the project. As the estimate of the real cost of the project fluctuates with time, the contract price may or may not be modified.

In addition to the internal budget, an externally-funded project will have a contract price, or external budget, associated with it. Although the contract price and internal budget are loosely tied to each other, the relationship is not necessarily linear. In other words, the internal budget represents the real cost of the project, which by definition will be absorbed by the internal client; although modification of the contract price is a business decision tempered by client relation considerations, market conditions, and clauses of the contract at hand.

The business and contractual nuances of the project will temper the progress reporting, and more so the conversations that the project manager might have with the external client. These business features impart a delicate nature to the communication and relationship lines of the project manager. This relationship is rendered delicate because managing the external client relationship, and business

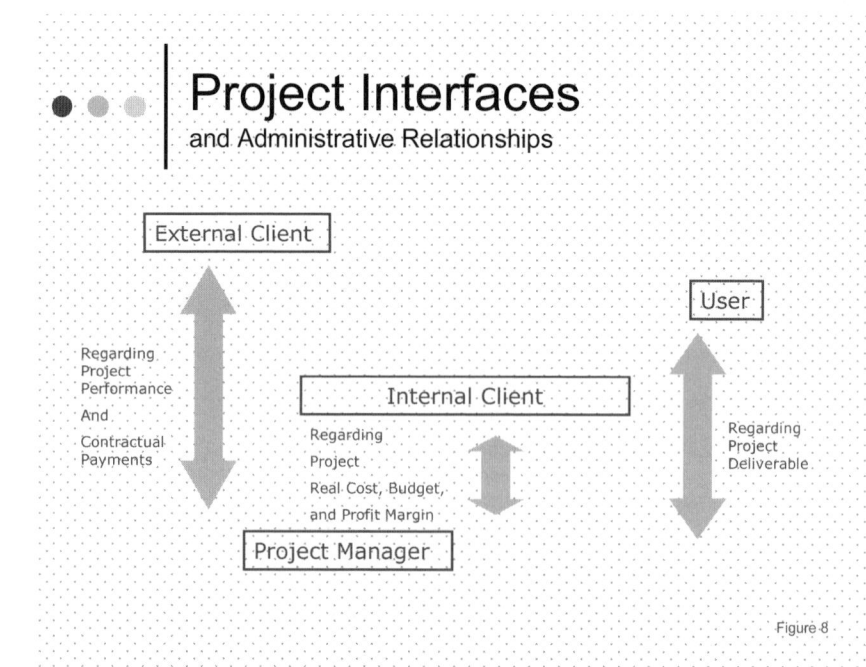

Project Interfaces
and Administrative Relationships

External Client

Regarding Project Performance And Contractual Payments

Internal Client

Regarding Project Real Cost, Budget, and Profit Margin

Project Manager

User

Regarding Project Deliverable

Figure 8

issues of the project, are added to the traditional project management activities of the project manager.

When dealing with the users of the project, the project manager will address the performance attributes of the deliverable. When conversing with, and reporting to, the external client, the project manager will address project performance and its corresponding contractual payments. When conversing with, and reporting to, the internal client, the project manager will address the real cost of the project, its corresponding internal budget, and the profit margin resulting from this project. (Figure 4-8)

4.3 Organizational Attitude Toward Projects

Every organization has the general goal of improving its operational efficiency, although not all organizations recognize that successful projects are the facilitative tools that ensure that organizations attain and maintain leadership in their fields. The transition to project management sophistication is difficult because it will require some monetary investment, and it will definitely require a culture change. Thus, among organizations that are poised for sophistication and excellence in project management, the pace at which an organization achieves the targeted sophistication will directly depend on how much time, effort, and support, is dedicated to the enhancement of project management processes, procedures, and tools.

Organizational project management sophistication is a function of competent individuals, harmonious teams, and a friendly organizational environment. Individual competence is usually manifested in gracefully handling the things aspects of project, such as cost, schedule, risk, scope, and quality. Productivity of the team can be observed in artful management of all aspects of people issues of the project, such as conflict management, communication, and team spirit. However, a team composed of such professionals, team managers and team members alike, will not be fully successful without the assistance and facilitation of a friendly and supportive organizational environment.

A friendly environment usually includes organizational infrastructure units whose missions are fostering project success through actively implementing best practices in project management. Some of the obvious manifestations of a project-friendly environment are that the organization provides procedures, forms, and sophisticated tools for the team members in order to assist the team perform their duties accurately, successfully, and rapidly. (Figure 4-9)

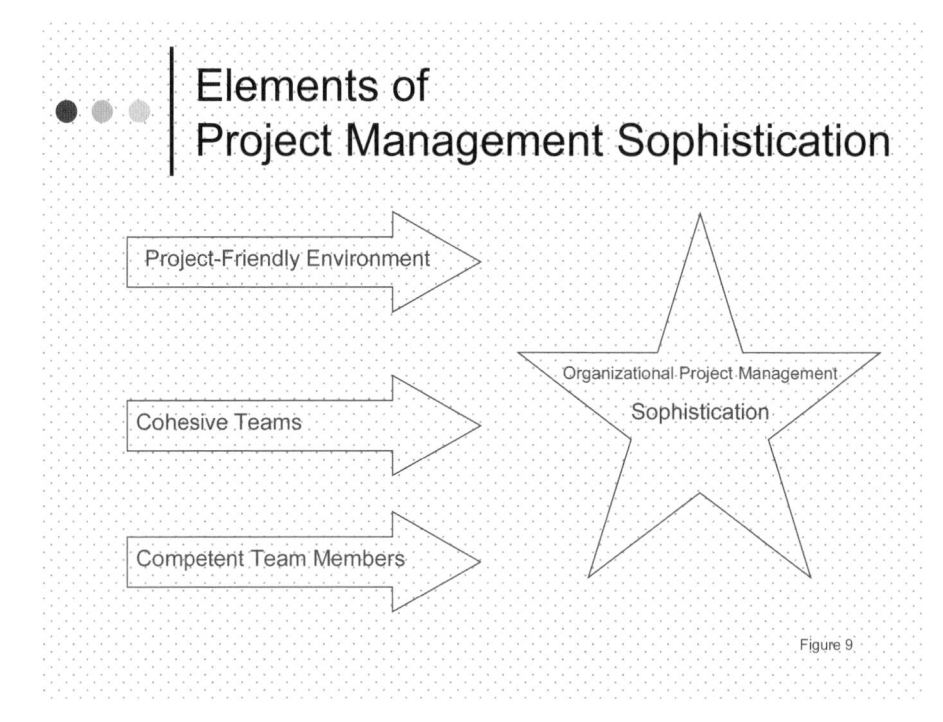

Elements of Project Management Sophistication

- Project-Friendly Environment
- Cohesive Teams
- Competent Team Members

Organizational Project Management Sophistication

Figure 9

A friendly environment is created when the upper executives ensure that the project has the right number of team members with the right competency. Further, in a project-friendly environment, the upper management provides to the team all of the tools and techniques that are necessary for proper execution of the project.

By contrast, traditional organizational structures are designed to protect the integrity and autonomy of the various functions of the organization. Consequently, they are friendly to ongoing functional activities and not to projects. Organizations that have operated under the traditional functional structure for a long time will require significant investments, and extensive culture change, to adopt an attitude of support and friendliness toward projects and to provide the required facilitative infrastructure for projects.

Project-friendly features of an organization are usually fostered through the establishment of a full scale Enterprise Project Management Office (EPMO). EPMO will provide tools and processes for developing refined and comprehensive estimates, schedules, and quality plans. EPMO will further provide tools and techniques for collecting meaningful progress information to be used for plan modification and for development of lessons learned for future projects. EPMO will also assure that there is always an amply supplied resource pool is available for newly commissioned projects. These comprehensive resource pools should include

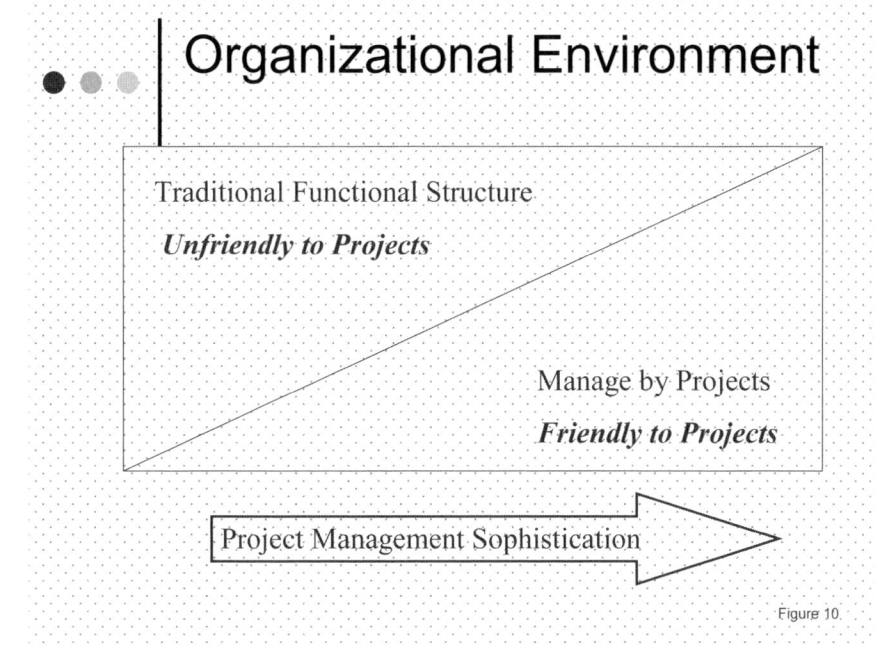

Organizational Environment

Traditional Functional Structure
Unfriendly to Projects

Manage by Projects
Friendly to Projects

Project Management Sophistication →

Figure 10

a fully-staffed cadre of well trained project management professionals, and a generous supply of equipment and materials. (Figure 4-10)

4.4 Management Structure

Probably one of the most common forms of organizational structure is that of hierarchical, which is often blended with micromanagement. This form of management structure is usually found in organizations that start out as a partnership of a few principals. These small and tight-nit organizations eventually tend to become very hierarchical and rank-based. This characteristic hands-on form of management by the upper executives is a definite advantage during the periods that the organization is in its infancy and is composed of only a few partners. However, as the organization grows, this form of management should be abandoned in favor of a management style that is more suitable for a larger organization. Sadly, this expectation does not always materialize.

The hierarchical form of management becomes the management style of choice in environments that experience high personnel turnover, and thus the members of the upper and middle management tend to be the stable source of a significant amount of organizational memory. Therefore, this operational mode tends to do very well with routine and repetitive work such as maintenance, security, manufacturing, etc.

Organizations that have operated under the micro-management principle tend to run reasonably harmoniously primarily because the members of the upper executive team are very comfortable micro-managing all of those operations that are in their jurisdiction. Incoming executives learn very quickly that for things to get done, the executives will have to use personal involvement. Likewise, the existing employees are very comfortable in asking for, and accepting, advice and direction, for just about everything, from the upper executives; something that incoming employees will have to learn very quickly.

There is undisturbed operational harmony only if both the upper executives and employees subscribe to the same management philosophy. However, serious operational instabilities can develop if one of the upper executives subscribes to one philosophy while his/her staff subscribe to the other. New upper executives that have a tendency to delegate a lot of the work in their units, and employees whose work habits are founded on taking charge and being responsible for their own deliverable, will find working in a micro-managed environment professionally unsatisfying. These two groups, not being able to change the operational mode of a large organization, will ultimately leave. (Figure 4-11)

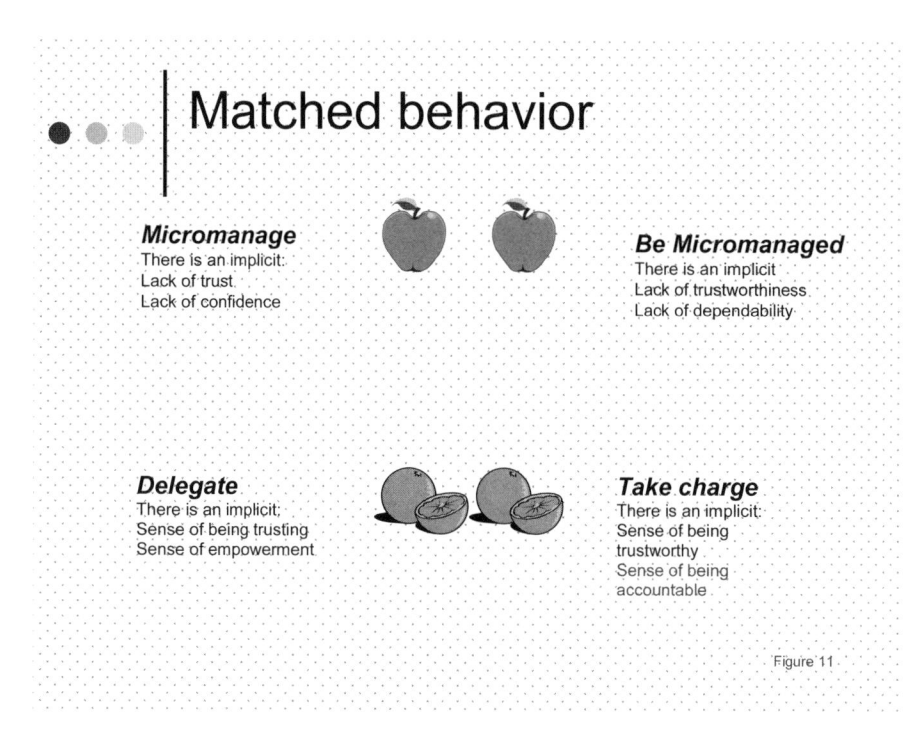

Matched behavior

Micromanage
There is an implicit:
Lack of trust
Lack of confidence

Be Micromanaged
There is an implicit
Lack of trustworthiness
Lack of dependability

Delegate
There is an implicit:
Sense of being trusting
Sense of empowerment

Take charge
There is an implicit:
Sense of being trustworthy
Sense of being accountable

Figure 11

One of the interesting side-effects of a micromanaging environment is that, since an upper executive does not have the time to monitor the activities of every project and every department, the executive would hire dotted-line staff members who, on behalf of their respective executive, will monitor and modify the activities of the entire jurisdiction that is assigned to that executive. Therefore, although the project members and line employees might hear the executive's name often, they will neither see him/her nor get direct instructions from him/her. The instructions will come indirectly through these surrogates. Indirect management is one of the classic symptoms of micromanagement on a large scale. Accordingly, a quick indication of the span of influence of an upper executive's micromanagement practices is to compare the population of his/her so called executive staff to the executive staffs of other executives.

A micro management mode of operation will stifle creativity on the part of the staff and, for better or for worse, places the burden of innovations and day-to-day problem-solving directly on the proverbial shoulder of the upper executives. The staff will either ask the upper executives what should be done in the face of an emerging situation or, worse yet, wait to be told what to do. At the other end of the spectrum, the delegation mode of operation will allow the staff to become creative, innovative, and responsive to the emerging problems of projects. In the delegation mode, the staff will either recommend and then take action or, better yet, solve the

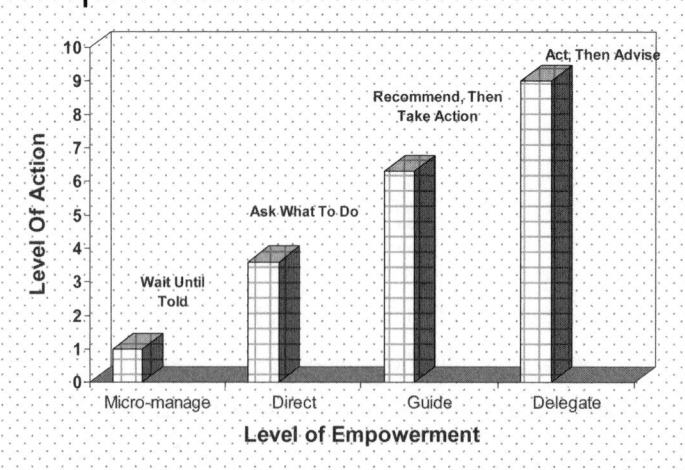

Leadership Spectrum

Figure 12

problem and then advise the project manager and upper executives of the novel solution that remedied that specific emerging problem. (Figure 4-12)

The predominant mode of management for a creativity-based organization should be that of delegation. Admittedly, this concept is almost diametrically opposite to what is normally practiced in unsophisticated organizations. In a typical unsophisticated organization, one might find a lot of instances where the upper executives practice micro-management in just about every facet of the organizational operations. This practice is euphemistically called hands-on, detail-oriented, personal involvement, and the personal-touch. Probably a classic symptom of an unsophisticated organization is that many projects will have to have an executive sponsor for their survival, and that the project can not be approved based on its own merits. Subscribing to the sponsor concept is simply an admission that a project is pursued not because its deliverable is perceived to be crucial to the success of the organization, but rather it is being approved on the basis of the personality, charisma, and debating skills of its sponsor.

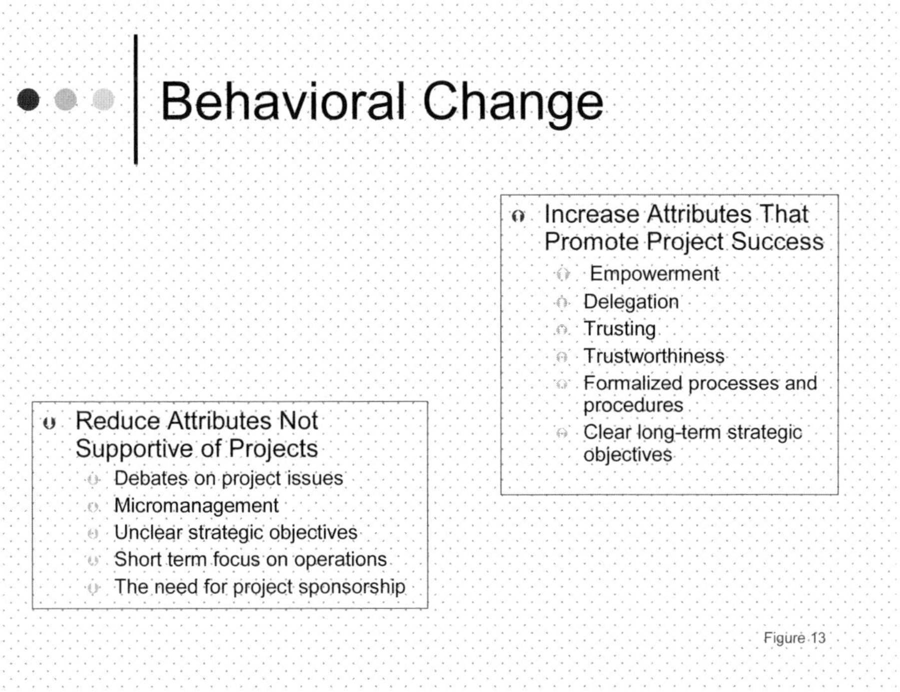

Behavioral Change

- Increase Attributes That Promote Project Success
    - Empowerment
    - Delegation
    - Trusting
    - Trustworthiness
    - Formalized processes and procedures
    - Clear long-term strategic objectives

- Reduce Attributes Not Supportive of Projects
    - Debates on project issues
    - Micromanagement
    - Unclear strategic objectives
    - Short term focus on operations
    - The need for project sponsorship

Figure 13

If an organization is determined to make the journey from unsophisticated to sophisticated in project management, and to modify the work environment to one that nurtures sophisticated project management work, there are certain organizational behavioral patterns that must be minimized, or eliminated. First and foremost, the amount of micro-management should be reduced and ultimately eliminated. Notable among other undesirable behavioral attributes are the hands-on pattern of conducting project selection, progress reporting. Lastly, the determination of project success should not be based on ad-hoc debates. (Figure 4-13)

Ideally, the upper management should focus on higher level objectives of the organization such as long range missions and market aspirations. In addition, the upper executives should express their vision for the organization explicitly and often, but the upper executives should stop short of getting involved in implementing those visions. Instead, The visions of the upper executives will be implemented by project management personnel expeditiously and judiciously.

Naturally, the pre-requisite for this process is that the upper management has created an environment conducive or loyalty, positive people relationships, self sufficiency, and trust. Further, one point that might appear to be counter-intuitive in micromanaging organizations is that project management maturity, first in class, and superior profits will occur naturally; if the organization focuses on project-friendly structures for the organization, and project management sophistication for the operations.

The issues of micromanagement and trust, or lack thereof, are closely tied to each other. To elaborate, if the upper executives could develop trust for project managers and project teams, then there would not be a need for as many intermediate review milestones for projects. If one looks at the master schedule of a project, internally-funded or externally-funded alike, one would find a large number of intermediate review milestones. In the vast majority of cases, these milestones are not necessary for the logical conduct of the project, but rather they represent the lack of trust in the project team. These milestones provide opportunities for upper management to micromanage the project, and opportunities for the project team to verify their instructions for the conduct of the next leg of the project.

This lack of trust, and the existence of micromanagement, is also manifested by multi-signature approval processes for project initiation, and for major project decisions. The multi-signature process refers to the ritual by which the original plan, and the subsequent changes to that plan, of the project will be authorized. The project manager prepares the plans and signs the bottom of the approval sheet; and submits them to his/her manager for approval. Once the manager signs the form, then it gets forwarded to the next level of the chain of command for approval. It is typical that a project document will have to be approved by seven levels of management, as signified by as many signatures on the approval sheet, before the document is considered to have been authorized.

An interesting side-effect of this process is that the credit is shared, but so is the blame. In other words, it is not quite clear who should be applauded if the project is successful, and who should be held responsible if the project is not as successful as hoped. It would be no surprise to find out that the multi-signature-practice is one of the basic ingredients of the organizational apathy and cynicism. There is a dark-humor project management myth that only those people who had no significant input into the project get rewarded for the completion of the project, sometimes even if the project is a failure. If and when this hierarchical approval process was to be eliminated, or at least tempered, that would provide symbolic evidence that the upper executives trust the judgment, and appreciate the sacrifices, of the project team.

4.5 Project Management Professionals

Sophistication in project management will require the maximum possible incidents of delegation of authority to the project team for the discharge of project duties. Naturally, there is direct link between authority, responsibility, and accountability.

The first part of this direct link is that the upper management of the organization must extend the authority and responsibility, for the implementation of the project, to the project manager and the team. The second part of the link is that the upper executives will hold the project manager, and the project team, accountable for the success of the project. In such an environment, project team members would be empowered to take innovative actions to solve emerging project problems or to conduct continuous improvement in project processes. These enhancements will not only benefit the project at hand, by also will positively impact the conduct of all of the future projects of the organization.

It is generally accepted that, for the purposes of authority and operational efficiency, the project manager of an externally funded project should be treated as the CEO of that small temporary enterprise, which is the project. The increase in outsourcing, and the increase in the use of global projects in both internally-funded and externally-funded projects, provides a more widespread use for this concept. Thus, in the performing organizations, each project is assigned to a project manager whose professional performance is measured directly by the success of the project, just like a CEO. This concept is manifested by the notion that the project manager is directly responsible for the success of the project, through detailed planning, skillful execution, and tactful scope change requests. Interestingly enough, in these organizations, the upper management of the performing organization will govern the project, in a fashion similar to how the board of directors of an organization governs the CEO. Many organizations practice this concept without verbalizing or labeling the specifics of the behavior. Lastly, it is entirely possible that, if the deliverable assigned to the project manager is relatively small, the significance of the CEO concept will be substantially diminished.

Ideally, the organization should select highly qualified and motivated project professionals for employment. The organization will train these project management professionals in the formalized processes of the organization, and familiarize them with the project-friendly features of the organization. Then, once these professionals are assigned to a project, they know precisely the extent of the tools and facilitative infrastructure the organization has put at their disposal. They will also be aware of the fact that they are fully in charge of, and responsible for, the success of the project. The last phase of this cycle is monitoring the stellar progress of these employees in implementing the project, and rewarding them accordingly. Naturally, s sophisticated organization will have specific guidelines as to how to measure and report project success, in totality or in individual elements of the deliverable. One simplified, and admittedly colloquial and conversational, way of describing the steps of the process is to recite the following: get good people, provide detailed direction, provide facilitative infrastructure, delegate, empower, get out of the way, and watch them succeed. (Figure 4-14)

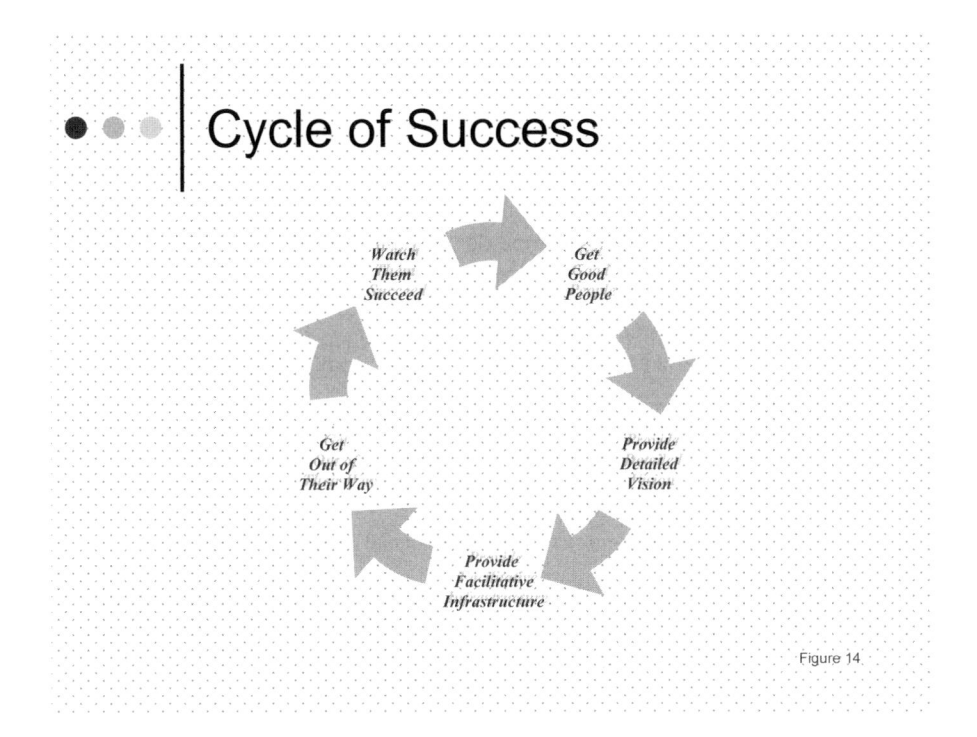

Cycle of Success

- Watch Them Succeed
- Get Good People
- Provide Detailed Vision
- Provide Facilitative Infrastructure
- Get Out of Their Way

Figure 14

In the same fashion that the project manager should be given the ample amount of authority for the conduct of the project, a commensurate amount of accountability should be assigned to the individual project team members. In cases of superior performance of the project, and hopefully there are frequent occasions of that, the project manager should be rewarded for the performance of the project. Given that delivery of the project as a whole is the result of team effort, each of team members should be rewarded for the success of the project also. To carry that one step further, and with the hopeful expectation that the project has detailed deliverable WBS, the project team members should be rewarded for the accuracy of the estimate and clarity of schedule of their respective components. The team members should also be recognized and rewarded for hard work, dedication, high quality deliverables, and continuous improvement in their respective areas and the entire project. (Figure 4-15)

Reward Structure
For Project Manager and Team Members

- Reward
  - Accurate and methodical estimate
  - Logical and workable schedule
  - Stellar quality
  - Continuous improvement
  - Hard work, dedication, loyalty, commitment

  - Reward project manager for
    - Project success
  - Reward team members for
    - Project success
    - Success of elements assigned to each member

Figure 15

A project-friendly organization must have an identifiable reward-and-recognition structure for project management professionals in order to encourage project teams to perform at their peak. An additional feature of a sophisticated environment is that the upper management will give proper recognition to the project management personnel who have shown stellar performance, in managing projects, programs, and proposals. Thus, project management professionals will have the assurance that their performance will not go unnoticed, and they will use their innovative and operational skills to deliver successful project. The recognition can be in monetary terms such as a salary increase, bonus, award, or even a paid-dinner for the team member's family. Non-monetary rewards can be honorable mention at the departmental meeting, a plaque, a medal, or a title such as the employee of the month. Literature cites many instances where the professional employees regard recognition to be as important as, and sometimes to be more important than, financial rewards.

Finally, in lump sum contracts/projects, and in internally-funded projects, there is a tradition that the project team members are asked to work additional hours on the project in an overtime fashion. Sometimes, these additional hours are exerted without a formal compensation. There should mechanisms in place that would record the actual time that was spent by the project team on the project in order to collect real and meaningful project historical data. Then, the real resource expenditures of the project should be preserved for use by models that are used to plan and estimate future projects. Not to be forgotten is that guidelines must be in place to provide financial and non-financial rewards for those team members who chose to work long hours to bring the project back on track. These gestures are among the many that would symbolize the organizational attitude toward continued loyalty, and toward organizational recognition of dedicated work.

4.6 Project Management Career Track

An organization which is friendly to projects will regard project management as a bona-fide profession, and not as an accidental profession, nor as a title that will be bestowed upon someone without considerations to the person's duties and skills. In general, efforts should be made to elevate project work as glamorous as functional work, maybe even more so. Accordingly, there must be well-defined career tracks that are specifically focused on project management activities.

One would hope that the performing organization has a large cadre of talented project management professionals for the full spectrum of project management tasks. Nonetheless, as an organization grows, and as there is the inevitable personnel turnover, there must be processes in place in order to blend the incoming employees into the current project management resource pool. Additionally, there must be a schema in place with which all of the staff members are trained and encouraged to undertake more advanced functions. Project management professionals should be allowed to accumulate experience in small or routine projects before they are assigned to complex projects.

Further, the career ladder of project management professionals must have two major dimensions: traditional collocated projects and virtual projects. Naturally, exposure to traditional collocated projects should precede exposure to global or virtual projects. Assignment to virtual projects should also consider personal

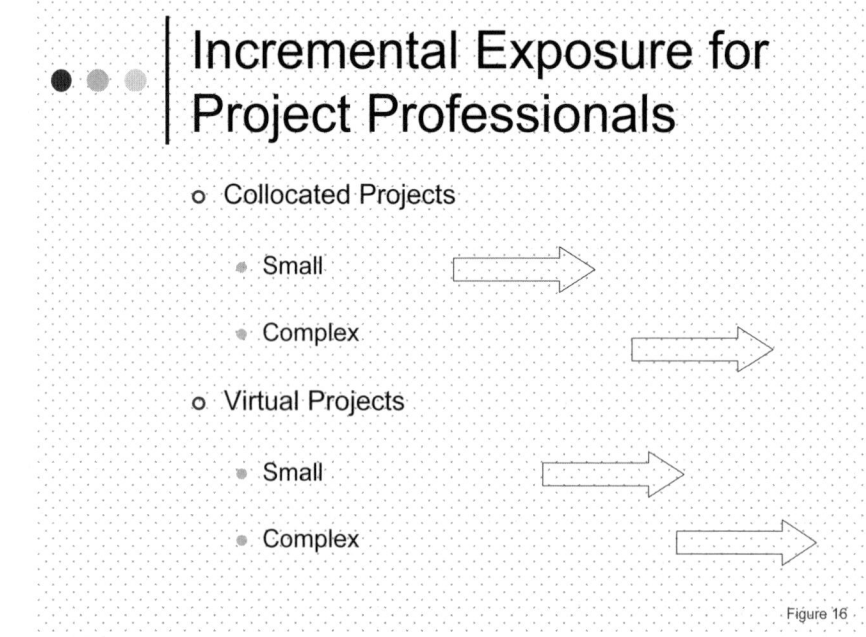

Incremental Exposure for Project Professionals

- Collocated Projects
  - Small
  - Complex
- Virtual Projects
  - Small
  - Complex

Figure 16

behavioral patterns and preferences. There is a group of people that would feel more comfortable in a face-to-face mode of operation, and they get motivated and energized by the direct interaction with other team members; if at all possible, these people should be principally assigned to traditional projects. By comparison, there is a group of people that would feel more comfortable in dealing with others through written documents and through the internet, and who are self-motivated and self-regulated; these people should be given preference for assignment to virtual projects. (Figure 4-16)

There is a fundamental difference between the duties of project managers and the duties of project team members. Project managers tend to spend only a small fraction of their time on technical tasks, and far more on project management tasks. In a well running organization, no more than 10% of the team's effort should be spent on project management. By contrast, project team members tend to spend the vast majority of their time on technical issues. Therefore, the process for promoting project team members to the project manager position should be such that competence in technical area is not the only requirement for elevation to the rank of project manager.

The career ladder of the project management professional should have enough flexibility such that only those who enjoy technical work continue to work as team members, while only those who enjoy project management work will be advanced to assume project manger duties as part of their chosen advancement steps. This flexibility should provide not only titles and staff grade to recognize the team member's experience, but also sufficient compensation so that the team member is not penalized for choosing either route. Under this plan, project management professionals are placed in positions that are professionally rewarding, while maximizing their productivity. Lastly, elevation to project manager of a virtual team should not only be preceded by having served as the project manager of a traditional collocated project, but also be dependent upon the personal inclinations of the prospective project manager in question. (Figure 4-17)

Increasing Responsibility for Project Team Members

- Collocated Projects
  - Member →
  - Manager ⟹
- Virtual Projects
  - Member →
  - Manager ⟹

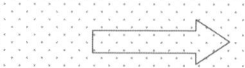

Figure 17

There is a distinct group of project managers, who are very charming, and can be very persuasive; these project managers can be described as charismatic project managers. These project managers are often rewarded for their projects, primarily as a result of their personality, and not necessarily as a result of the definitive success of their projects. They tend not to do any formal planning because the implementation of their project, and the execution of the change management functions of those projects, tends to be successful primarily due to their charming personalities.

The charismatic project managers should be placed as project managers of collocated projects because they tend to do well in face to face interactions, and understandably they tend not to do well in the virtual environment. Further, the organization might opt to assign charismatic project managers to duties that require a lot of interaction, and a substantial amount of face-to-face negotiations. Naturally, even then, the charismatic project managers should be encouraged to subscribe to formalized project management, which has now become the organizational norm.

To put the full spectrum of project management duties in perspective, a project management professional should be given the opportunity for skill-enhancement and career-advancement in all facets of the tasks available within the organization. The project manager of the prospective project should be permitted and encouraged to pursue a career track that would maximize his/her abilities toward his/her professional satisfaction, while making significant contributions toward the best interests of the organization. In other words, although an incoming staff member will initially be assigned the technical duties of a simple collocated project, the staff member should be given the opportunity to transition to different modes of project management work as his/her skills and personal inclinations warrant. In addition to pursuing a technical competence track, the career tracks available to a project manager professional would be managing collocated teams and managing virtual teams. Beyond that, the career options would include serving on, or managing, the teams that handle proposals, programs, or portfolios. (Figure 4-18)

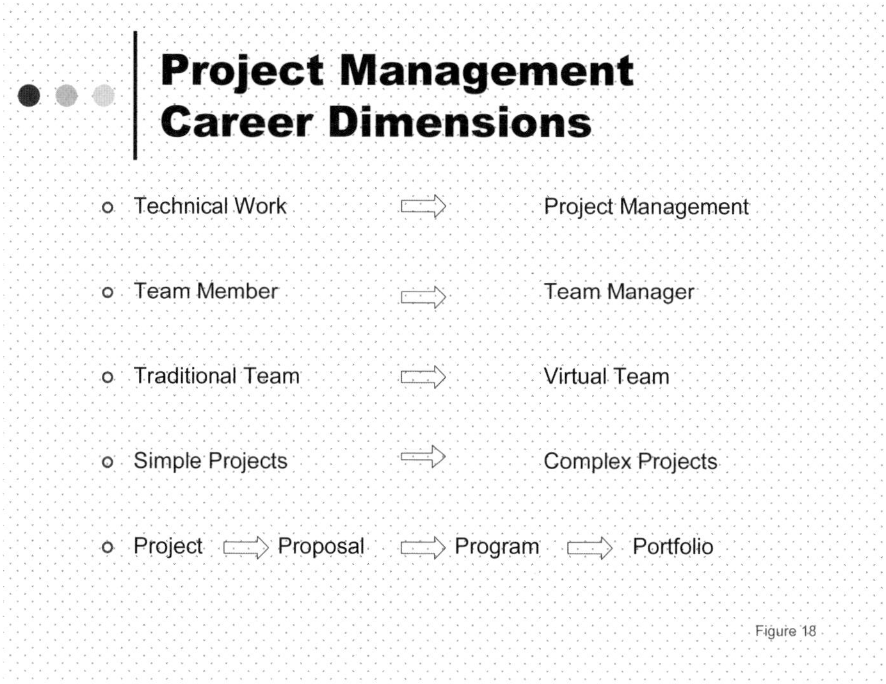

Project Management Career Dimensions

- Technical Work ⇒ Project Management
- Team Member ⇒ Team Manager
- Traditional Team ⇒ Virtual Team
- Simple Projects ⇒ Complex Projects
- Project ⇒ Proposal ⇒ Program ⇒ Portfolio

Figure 18

4.7 Staffing Considerations

When a project is initiated, the first step would involve assigning the needed number of professionals, with the appropriate skills, to that project. Additionally, the team should be given all of the material and equipment resources that it needs for an expeditious execution of the project. A sophisticated organization will be able to match the project with the most qualified personnel effectively and seamlessly, because a sophisticated organization is fully aware of the capabilities of all of its staff members. When assigning project team members to a project, personality matching would streamline the team building efforts of the project team.

Project managers and team members should not be assigned to projects on a part time basis, particularly if the optimum performance of the project requires full time engagement. Part time assignment not only thwarts the project progress, but it has the undesirable side effect that it promotes treating project work as secondary and a nuisance. It is symptomatic that organizations that are unfriendly to projects tend to assign only a fraction of the staff that would be necessary for a speedy completion of the project.

Further, project management professionals should not be assigned to several projects to create the illusion of having many ongoing projects, in which case, most of the projects tend to take a long time to complete. A typical case would be that, even though the organizational staff might be able to support only ten projects, the organization boasts on having thirty projects in the pipeline, sidestepping the fact that all of these projects will take up to four time longer to complete under this set of circumstances.

If the organization chooses to plan all of the projects based on the optimal performance of the team and the project, then there would be a finite number of projects that the project staff can support, and the portfolio of proposals/projects will limit the portfolio content to that finite number. If for some reason the staff size is smaller than the optimal size, then the organization can make a conscious decision of choosing one of the following: reduce the number of projects in the pipeline, or keep the number of projects the same with the understanding that the delivery date for all or some of the projects will be delayed.

This balance between the client convenience and organizational convenience has analogues in other industries. Probably the most notable analogy is that of providing the number of toll takers in a toll plaza. The management's conscious choice could be to have the customers go through the toll plaza without waiting, while some of the toll-takers might be idle. At the other end of the spectrum, there is a long line of cars at all staffed toll booths (making the customer wait) while assuring that all toll takers are fully occupied. These two distinctly-different situations can be characterized as: one that favors the convenience of the client, whereas the latter favors the convenience of the performing organization. (Figure 4-19)

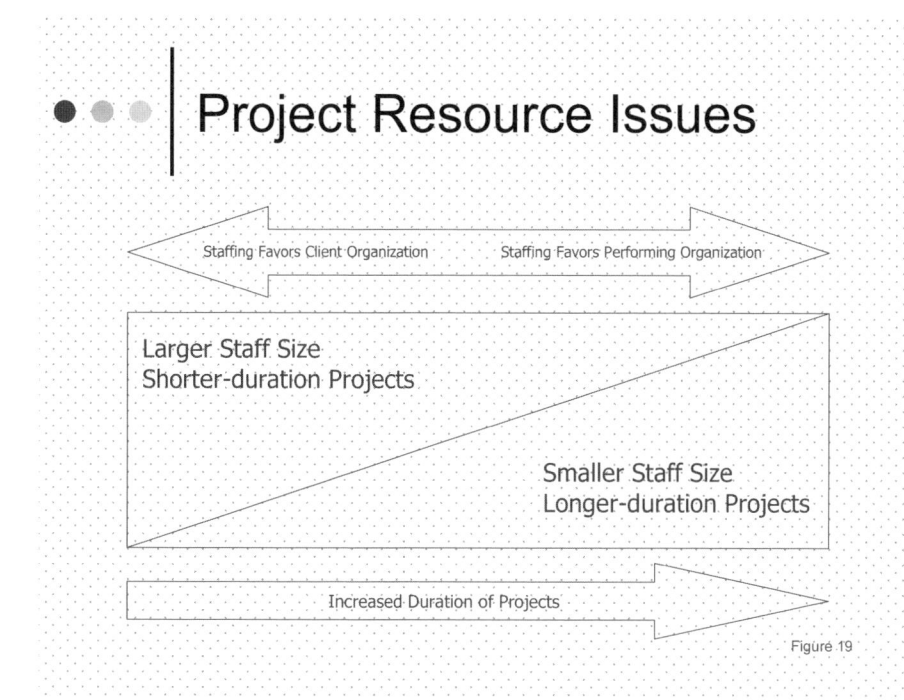

Project Resource Issues

Staffing Favors Client Organization ⟷ Staffing Favors Performing Organization

Larger Staff Size
Shorter-duration Projects

Smaller Staff Size
Longer-duration Projects

Increased Duration of Projects →

Figure 19

This mode of project staffing might create possible standby time for project management professionals. If there are more people resources than are needed by projects, then the standby staff can be assigned to projects very quickly; trademark of a client-focused organization. On the other hand, if there are more projects than people, then this would be a resource-focused organization, causing delays for the projects.

Given that it is near to impossible to guarantee that at all times all projects are fully staffed, and all of the staff is assigned, the organization must make a conscious choice of which mode of operation it is planning to pursue. If the performing organization chooses to create a client-focused project environment, then there needs to be a mechanism of handling the staff standby time during those periods that there is an excess of project staff. There are a multitude of productive tasks that can be performed by these professionals during these so called standby times; all of these tasks will benefit the long-term project management sophistication of the organization. The staff members who are on standby, can help draft procedures and

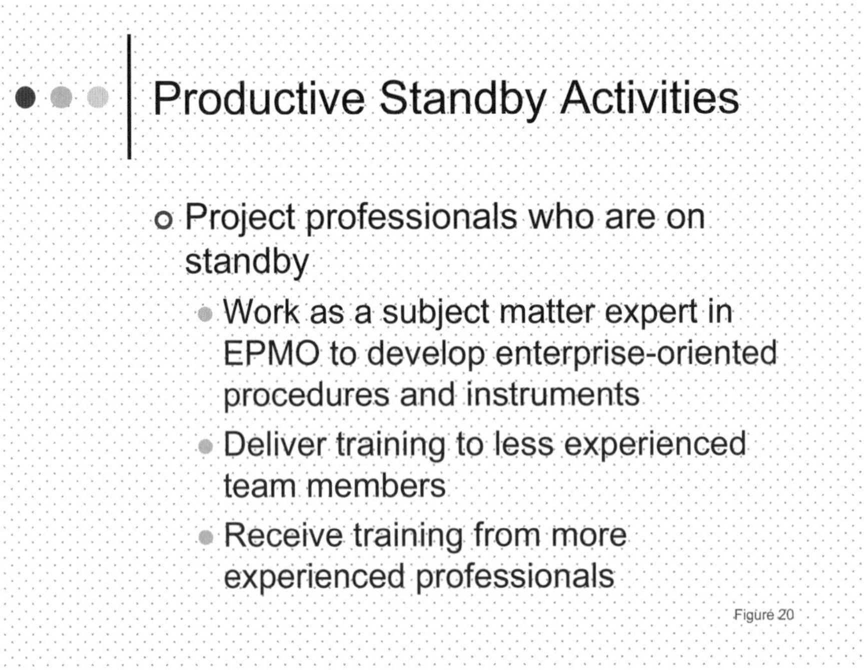

Productive Standby Activities

- Project professionals who are on standby
  - Work as a subject matter expert in EPMO to develop enterprise-oriented procedures and instruments
  - Deliver training to less experienced team members
  - Receive training from more experienced professionals

Figure 20

guidelines on behalf of the EPMO, they could deliver training on the subjects of their expertise to less experienced project staff, or they themselves could attend training course in their areas of competency deficiency. (Figure 4-20)

Chapter Summary During the performance phase of the contract, the project team will refine the project plans before starting the full scale execution of the project plans. The performance of the project, and by extension the performance of the contract, will be greatly enhanced if the project management professionals were afforded trust, loyalty, and an environment that is friendly to projects. Once variances to the project in the areas of cost, schedule, and scope, present themselves, the project manager and the upper management of the performing organization must make the painful decision of whether to absorb the remedial costs internally or to request payment for those cost-increases from the external client.

5. Contract Modification Phase

During the execution phase of the project, the project team will make every attempt to minimize the cost of the project while maintaining acceptable levels for the duration of the project, for the quality, and for the scope of the deliverable. The process is composed of the revolving phases of developing the estimate for cost and duration, establishing the budget, managing the inevitable changes to the project plans, and making modifications to the estimate and schedule baseline.

Beyond efforts to fine-tune the project plans, there are almost innumerous reasons for the changes that occur in the various aspects of the project during its implementation. The causes of change will fall into two major categories: those changes whose costs will be reimbursed by the client organization and those changes whose costs will be absorbed by the performing organization. A change order is the official request mechanism for modifying the contractual baseline in concert with the current project predictive data.

If the changes can be traced to the client organization's actions or instructions, then they are possibly reimbursable. The reimbursable incremental costs can be the results of scope and schedule changes that were initiated by the client organization, in turn as a result of changes in strategic needs. The reimbursable changes could also include those brought on by unexpected deleterious site conditions, by technological upgrades, and by evolutions in design philosophy.

On the other hand, the absorbed incremental costs are those that can not be directly linked to any modifications that might have been initiated by the client organization; not easily anyhow. Usually, these incremental costs can be attributed to the performing organization's actions or non-actions. If the incremental cost is the result of errors of the performing organization in design, cost estimate, schedule network, and implementation practices, they are clearly non-reimbursable. Debates between the client organization and the performing organization during the modification phase usually tend to revolve around whether a particular change falls into the reimbursable category or into the non-reimbursable category. These debates might become heated and occasionally they result in contentious litigation between the two parties. (Figure 5-1)

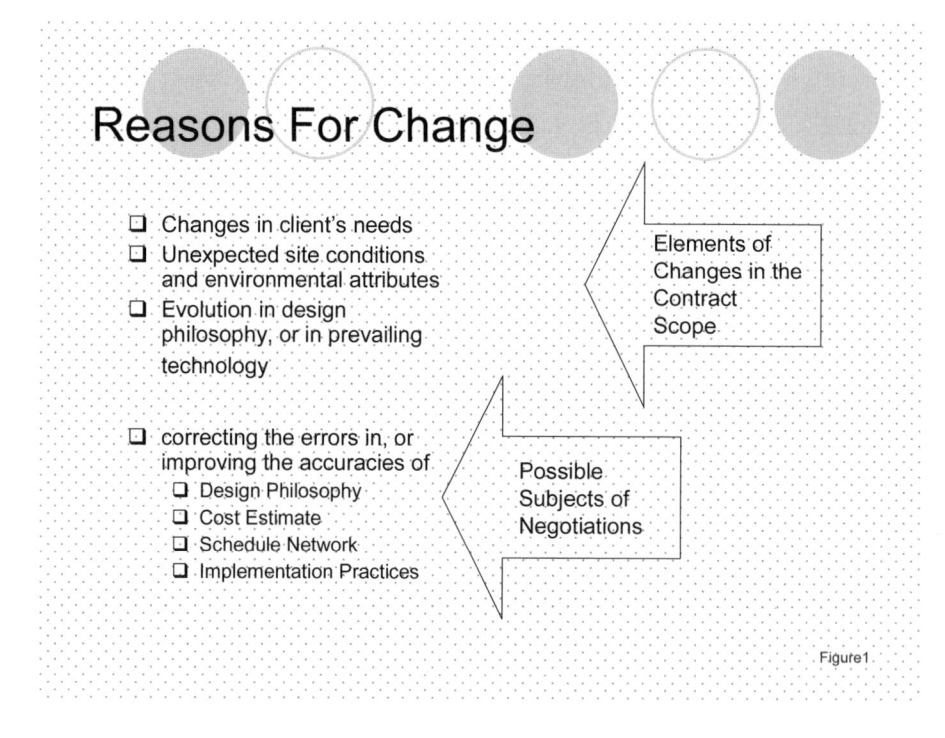

Reasons For Change

- Changes in client's needs
- Unexpected site conditions and environmental attributes
- Evolution in design philosophy, or in prevailing technology

Elements of Changes in the Contract Scope

- correcting the errors in, or improving the accuracies of
  - Design Philosophy
  - Cost Estimate
  - Schedule Network
  - Implementation Practices

Possible Subjects of Negotiations

Figure 1

In most cases, the discrepancies in quality will be remedied at the expense of the performing organization without question. Further, many of the variances in cost, schedule, and scope, might be absorbed by the performing organization without any fanfare. However, major baseline changes will have to be implemented with client organization's concurrence, and will possibly be paid by the client organization.

The performing organizations usually have a threshold for the variances in cost. In circumstances that the cost of remedying variances in quality and schedule fall below the threshold, the cost of remedy can be absorbed by the performing organization. On the other hand, if the cost variance falls above the threshold, the additional cost will be presented to the client organization for approval and/or payment for remedies.

Even if the estimates of cost and duration were reasonably accurate based on the detailed information available at the time of the early plan, it is very likely that implementation cost and duration will not match the planned cost and duration due to unexpected occurrences. It is a reasonable expectation that the estimate of the total real cost of the project might vary with every estimate update. If a definitive budget is established from an early inaccurate estimate, the internal client, and hopefully the external client, will be sensitive to the precision limitations of the estimate. In other words, the project estimate, at least the internal component of it, should be treated as a living document, and updated as frequently as possible.

Experienced project managers are fully aware of the fact that treating the internal budget as in immovable object does not prevent cost and schedule variations of the project; it simply discourages good record keeping, and makes unavailable the data that might have isolated and explained the very likely future cost/schedule overruns. Therefore, as soon as the variance between the current and forecasted cost and duration values exceed the threshold set by the project team, the project team should request that the internal budget be adjusted to the then-current value of the estimate of the real cost.

During the negotiations involved in presenting the variances of the project to the client organization, and requesting funding from the client organization for remedying these variances, the contractor organizations are keenly aware of, and sensitive to, the client relations aspect of the process. A certain amount of goodwill facilitate the approval of the project performance, and the approval of the additions to contract price by way of change orders. As a result, sometimes the changes are implemented according to client's wishes but there is no increase to the amount that the client will have to pay, even though the real cost of the project to the contractor organization might have been increased as a result of the changes. In some ways, absorbing these incremental costs of the changes is akin to making an investment in the client relations aspect of this project, with the hopeful expectation that the goodwill that was created as a result of this behavior will assist in securing future contracts from the client.

During the execution phase, the goal of the project team is to maintain the most current baseline that has been approved by the internal client. If for whatever reason, the forecast of the real cost of the project points to a higher level, then the project manager must ask for a new internal budget from the internal client on the basis of the changes in the real cost of the project. Otherwise, the project will over-run its budget. In a way, this practice can be considered the de-facto mode of changing the budget baseline.

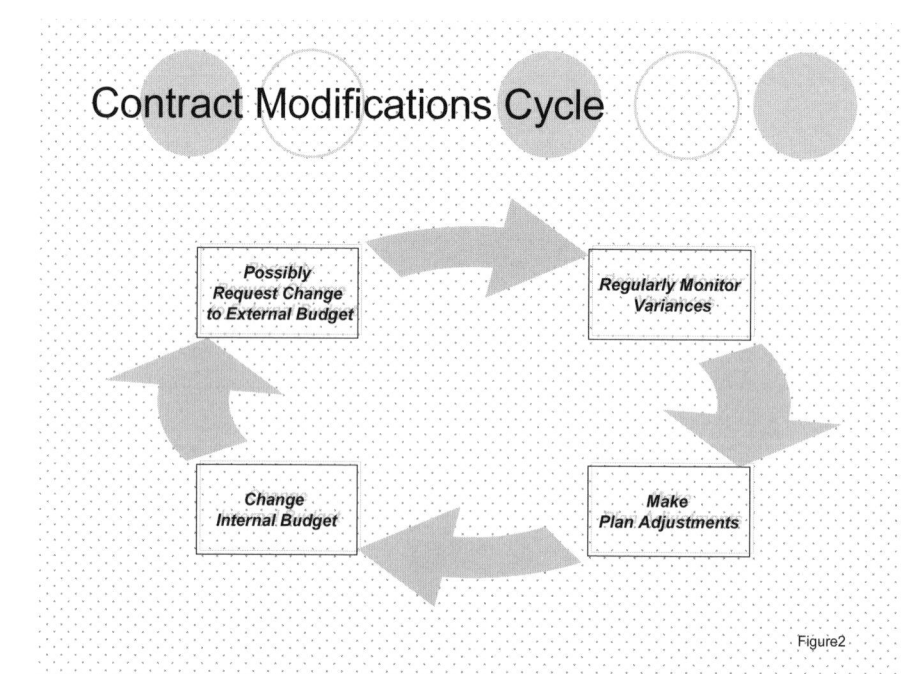

Contract Modifications Cycle

- Possibly Request Change to External Budget
- Regularly Monitor Variances
- Make Plan Adjustments
- Change Internal Budget

Figure2

Beyond that, the project manager might or might not ask for the approval of a new contract price from the external client. If due to the specifics of the circumstance, the contract price stays unchanged, the profit margin will be impacted negatively, because the real cost has increased just the same. Although the project manager is expected to maintain both the internal and external baselines, the project manager has less of a control over the means that are available to maintain the external baseline. Even with respect to the internal budget, maintaining baseline signifies the attempt on the part of the project team to stay within those boundaries. (Figure 5-2)

The relationship between the project manager, the upper management of the performing organization, and the external client, can sometimes be complex and very delicate. During the implementation of the contract price baseline change, the project manager must be mindful of his/her delicate relationships with the internal client and the external client. One of the instances where this relationship will be highlighted is when the real cost of the project is increased, but not necessarily the contract price.

Relationship Between Real Cost of Changes and Change Orders

New Price For External Client

Indirect connection to real cost
A business decision

New Budget For Internal Client

Direct connection
Based on REAL current cost estimate
Including the cost of changes

New Cost Estimate for the project

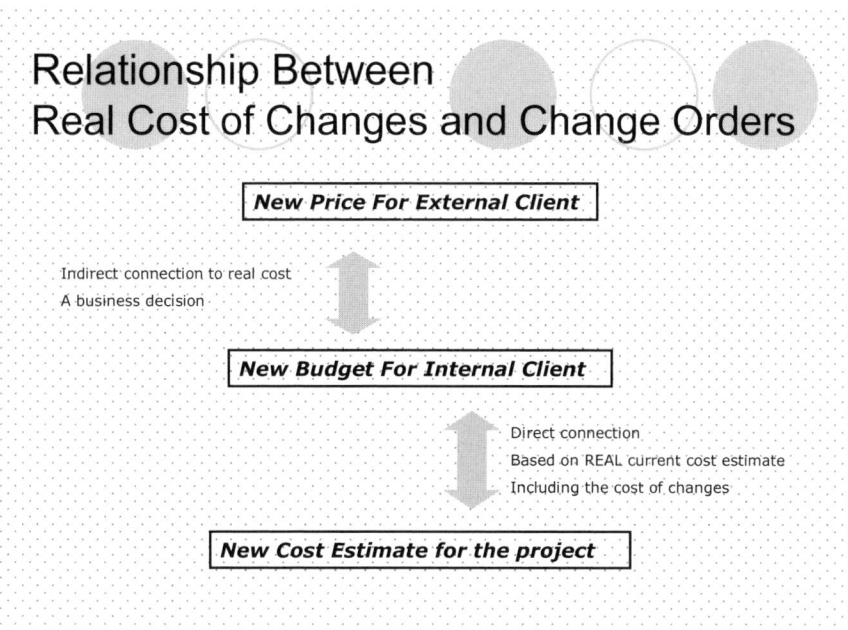

Figure 3

The project manager, in concert with the upper management of the performing organization, might choose to pass along the cost increase to the client. Alternately, the project manager, at the advice of the internal client, could choose to absorb the additional costs internally, thus reducing the profit margin of the organization, but hoping to gain an improvement in the goodwill of the client organization. The increase/decrease in the new contract price might or might not be directly proportional to increase/decrease in the real cost of the project. The modifications to contract price will be loosely based on the changes in real cost, as tempered by the client relation aspect of the project. (Figure 5-3)

Whether the client organization will choose to compensate the performing organization for the additional cost will be tempered by the type of contract that is in force for this project, the client relations considerations, and possibly the negotiation skills of the two parties. The attainment and retention of a goodwill with the client organization might be strained by the fact that one of the harsh realities of contracting is that sometimes it might be necessary to use litigation in order to change the duration of the project, to change the project's performance baseline, or to collect additional funds from the external client.

5.1 Accelerated Delivery Issues

During the implementation phase of the project, the project team will be placed in situations where the project team must make tradeoffs between cost, duration, and scope of the project. The process of making tradeoffs will be a consistent one if the project team, in consultation with the internal and external clients, has already established the ranking of cost, duration, and scope. The question to ask is that if it is imperative to make a choice between, say, cost and schedule, which one will have to take priority over the other. Put another way, the question to ask is which one will be more forgiving.

There is an interdependent relationship between the cost and the schedule of the project. This interdependence must be kept in mind when the changes in scope and specifications will necessitate changes in project cost and project schedule. The relationship between cost and schedule must be continually reviewed as the project evolves through its phases, when detailed project plans are formulated, when more definitive baselines are established, and finally when the inevitable tradeoffs must be made during the implementation phase of the project.

The traditional and simplest form of conducting projects is sequentially and by segments; one after another. This form of project execution minimizes the errors that can be introduced into the project deliverable due to rapid implementation, hasty communication, and workplace congestion. This pattern of sequencing the project segments has the feature that it produces the lowest cost of all options, although it takes the longest of all other scheduling options to complete the project. (Figure 5-4)

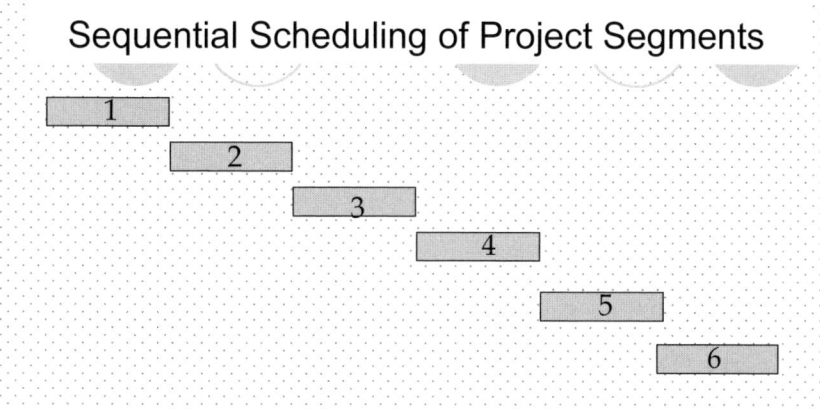

Sequential Scheduling of Project Segments

Traditions Sequencing Of Activities

Figure 4

There are occasions where the contract/project is progressing as planned, but the client organization's evolving needs now dictate an earlier delivery date. Another common circumstance for hastening the project pace is when the client expands the scope of the project, thus necessitating a longer duration for the project. Notwithstanding, the client might request that the contractor intensify the resource assignment such that the original delivery date will be maintained.

There are two ways of achieving a shorter duration for the project, by modifying the project scheduling network through sequencing of the various activities and segments, or by shortening the duration of the individual activities of the project.

The shorter duration for the project is achieved by breaking the project into as many segments as possible, and starting each segment as soon as possible and not necessarily after the full complement of the logical predecessor phase is completed. This technique is called fast tracking in construction projects, concurrent engineering in industrial and process projects, and rapid application development in software system development projects. It bears highlighting that a fast-track implementation schedule will require a larger number of people resources and equipment resources.

An example of the fast-track technique in the construction industry is, rather than wait until all components are designed before beginning the construction, the design documents are released in small increments so that construction of the facility can start well before the entire facility is fully designed. As such, the constructor will pour the concrete for the foundation while the design for the steel building frame is ongoing. An example of the rapid application development technique in the software industry is to begin developing individual components as soon as a discrete portion of the requirements is defined. Another example in the software industry is to test individual modules as they are developed, rather than waiting to test all components together when the software development is fully complete. It bears highlighting that testing individual modules, one at a time, may not be as cost effective as testing all the modules at the same time, and while testing the integrated product.

The incentive in using the method of overlapping segments is that, if the project is implemented smoothly, the delivery date is far more attractive. Unfortunately, there is an inherent drawback in overlapping those phases that are logically serial phases. Therefore, it is fair to say that this expectation does not always materialize. When such phases are overlapped, the resource intensity impact, the cost impact, and even the schedule impact of recovery from errors and reworks are somewhat drastic; this cost increase is commonly referred to as the cost of errors. (Figure 5-5)

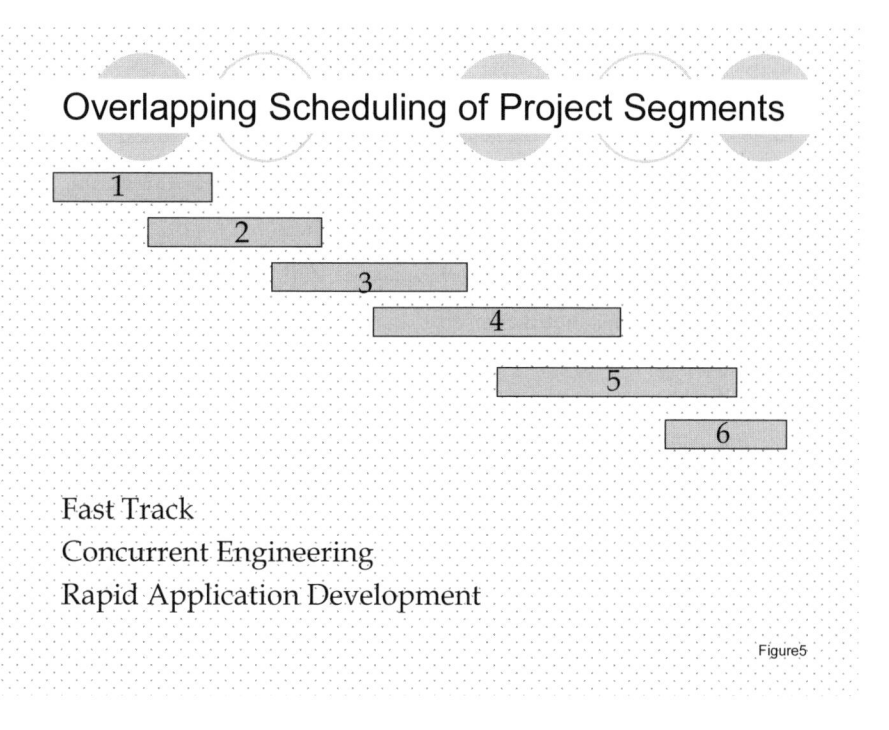

Overlapping Scheduling of Project Segments

1
2
3
4
5
6

Fast Track
Concurrent Engineering
Rapid Application Development

Figure5

The second means of reducing the project duration will involve compressing the critical path of the project, and that is achieved, not by reducing the number of activities in the chain, but rather by compressing selected activities of the critical path. Compressing individual critical path activities would involve adding more shifts or a larger crew size to a given activity in order to reduce the duration of that particular activity, and hence the project. Selection of activities for compression depends on three factors: by prioritizing critical path activities based on the costs associated with compressing an activity, by ranking them according to the risk associated with each activity compression, and by prioritizing these elements based on their impact on schedule. Needless to say, critical path elements will not be considered for compression if associated costs are prohibitive, the risk is too high, or the schedule impact is minimal.

Thus, compression of individual critical path activities will be accomplished through adding resources to each activity that is compressed. In a way, fast-tracking a project and compassing a single activity represent the same concept; with the distinction that one is at a small scale while the other is on a grand scale.

Since projects are intended to develop deliverables that must ultimately satisfy a specific business need, there is always a certain amount of pressure on the project team to finish the project sooner. Therefore, if the client wishes the project duration to be compressed, that is how the project manager will proceed, although everyone needs to be aware of the fact that project compression will carry a definitive and predictable cost penalty and an embedded risk for further cost increases.

Thus, it is important to be aware of the implications of compressing the duration of a project. As a rule of thumb, if the duration of the project is halved, the total effort for the project will double. In other words, there is always a cost penalty for reducing the project duration from what is considered to be the optimum. In construction projects, increasing the number of workers will cause physical congestion, which will cause slowdowns and potential safety hazards. In software projects, the detrimental effects of a larger crew are subtler and less visible, but present nonetheless.

Historical project data in several industries has shown that there is a minimum cost for each task and that this minimum cost will occur when the optimum crew size and optimum shift duration is implemented during the implementation of that task. Therefore, one would hope that the original project cost baseline is derived from the original elemental cost baseline, which in turn was developed using optimum crew size for the elements. By extension, the baseline duration is hopefully the optimum duration, because this baseline is also derived from the pristine baseline. Then, if a performance duration other than the optimum duration is chosen midstream for the project, the effects of such duration compression, or expansion, on cost can be determined methodically and consistently using a normalized curve depicting the relationship between cost and duration in that type of project. The cost-duration relationship can be applied equally well to individual tasks and the project as a whole. (Figure 5-6)

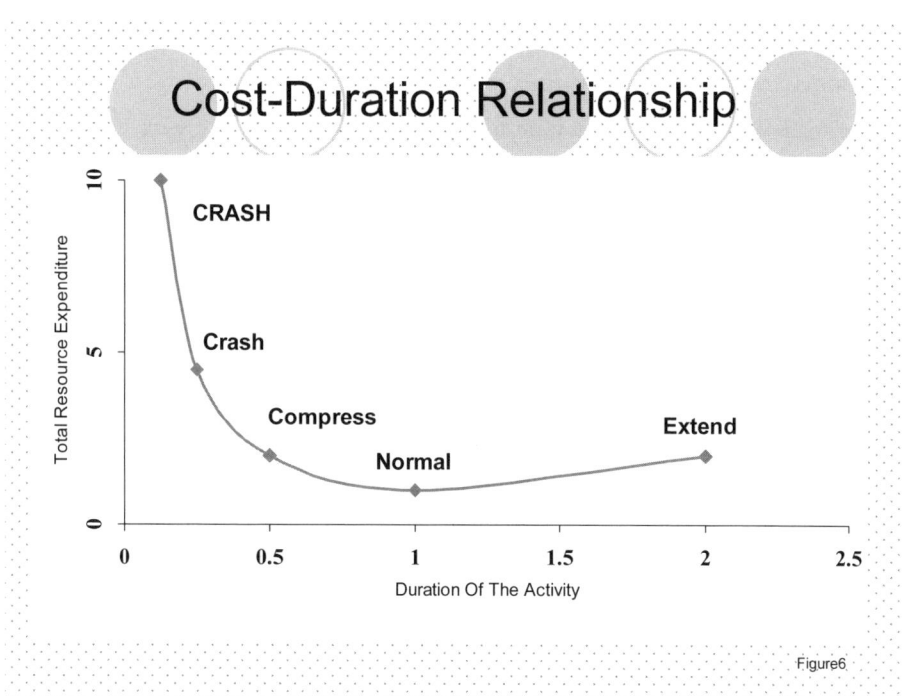

Cost-Duration Relationship

Total Resource Expenditure vs. Duration Of The Activity

- CRASH (at ~0.1, 10)
- Crash (at ~0.3, 4)
- Compress (at ~0.6, 2)
- Normal (at 1, 1)
- Extend (at 2, 2)

Figure6

There is a threshold beyond which project duration cannot be compressed. This threshold is normally about one half of the optimum duration of the project, and it is commonly referred to as the crash point. The goal in compressing projects is to compress project duration only to those durations that are longer than the crash

Modification Phase

point. Normally, clients ask for a 10% or 20% reduction in duration, assuming that the original duration was optimum, of course.

Ironically, sometimes it comes as a surprise to the clients, and even to some project managers, that when the crew size for an activity is increased in order to increase the pace of progress, the increased pace will be accompanied by a reduction in efficiency. This reduction in efficiency is due to hasty implementation, introduction of new unfamiliar team members to a task that is very time sensitive, and dramatic increases in communication errors, and duplication of work.

To illustrate the concept of optimum duration, consider an activity where it takes five programmers six days to develop the code for a particular database. If the duration is forced to four days, it might require nine programmers to finish this project. To extend this illustration to a point of extreme, if one were to force the duration to three days, twenty programmers would be required for the same task.

Illustrative Example
Activity Compression Penalty

Programmers	*Duration*	*Effort*
Five	Six Days	30 Worker Days
Seven	Five Days	35 Worker Days
Eleven	Four Days	44 Worker Days
Twenty	Three Days	60 Worker Days

Figure7.

At the other end of the spectrum, if there are resource shortages or cash flow constraints, then the project must be implemented with a smaller size, and less-than-optimum, crew in which case it will take longer to finish the project. This deviation from optimum will also increase the total effort of the project, although not as pronounced as compression would. If the duration is doubled, the total cost and effort will also double. The reduction in efficiency, which is caused by an increase in duration, is due to penalties involved in more-than-normal start-stop sequences of the processes, by reduced team interaction, and by deterioration in organizational and individual memory with respect to work details, and the loss of the learning curve effect. (Figure 5-7)

If the best option for a project, that is over-running its forecasts, is to maintain the original baseline for deliverable and the duration, then the variances in duration and scope can be implemented by expanding the size of the project team, or by outsourcing a portion of the project work through a sub-contract. Naturally, the details of this secondary outsourcing will have to be approved by the client organization, particularly if the client organization is expected to pay for the additional costs. Some clients insist on approving the people that get added to the project when there is a shortfall in the project schedule, even if the performing organization will bear the cost of these additional people.

Some project managers, particularly in the software and system development projects, anticipate, and react to, the possibility of network compression requests by embedding buffers in the original schedule logic. These embedded buffers are created during the planning stages by the inclusion of a lot of sequential activities, to be performed with an understaffed team, and using very few parallel activities. Then, once the client makes the all-expected request for duration compression, the project manager announces that some of the serial activities could now be done in parallel, and with the proper personnel, in order to accommodate the client's wishes; and that this can be done at minimal additional cost. This tactic, although very proactive and sometimes effective, can be highly explosive. If and when the client becomes aware that the original schedule, and the subsequent compression, were arbitrary, the project manager will lose all credibility and the effectiveness in explaining future project variances to the client. The best policy is to develop the original cost and schedule based on optimum crew size, cost, and duration. Then, as project circumstances such as skilled resource availability, and client business needs, present themselves, the budget and schedule will be changed accordingly.

Chapter Summary It is almost inevitable that there will be changes in the real cost, duration, or scope of a project during the implementation. Project managers and the project team must be prepared to deal with these changes. The contracting environment adds another dimension to this process. Once the real cost of a change has been determined, then there must be some debate as to whether the performing organization must absorb the cost of remedies, or the incremental cost should be passed along to the client organization.

6. Delivery Phase

The last phase of the project is called delivery phase in the contract documents; and it is called project closeout in the project management literature. The sophisticated performing organizations regard this phase as the most appropriate opportunity for setting the stage for future contracts from this client organization. Further, the collection of historical data, which is performed at this phase, will provide the foundation for improved planning and execution of future projects.

With the hopeful expectation that the just-finished project has been a positive experience for both client and performing organizations, usually the performing organization will use that experience as the foundation for acquiring future contracts from the same client organization. The premise is that the positive experience of this project will facilitate a better position for this performing organization during the prioritization of future proposals. Thus, positive behavioral attributes of the project personnel will not only result in a speedy payment for the current project, but might also become a positive historical reference for future projects.

Under normal circumstances, once the project is completed and the project product is delivered to the client organizations, the project/contract will be formally closed out. Under these circumstances, the project closeout is pleasant and predictable. However, there are those, hopefully-rare, cases where the project has to be terminated midstream. These unexpected terminations can be brought on by changes in the strategy of the client organization that authorized the project in the first place, by marginal quality of the project deliverable, or by project shortfalls in cost and schedule. Good client relations concepts dictate that the project manager should make every effort that the midstream project termination is not considered to be a reflection of the performance characteristics of the project team.

A view of success of a proposal/contract/project can be obtained by considering the execution phase of the project, in addition to the proposal development, of course. Thus, in performing organizations that engage in externally-funded projects, the overall success of the performing organization with respect to a project will be derived from two elements: the success of the proposal team in selecting that particular project for a proposal effort, and the success of the project team in the execution of the resulting project. In other words, the project is a success if the performing organization made all the right choices in selecting, and bidding on, that particular project; and if the organization continued to make all the right decisions during the execution of the project.

Organizations that are sophisticated in project management tend to encourage the project teams to conduct a comprehensive project planning, and a correspondingly careful project closeout. Detailed planning will provide a facilitative platform for

Project Close-out
Checklist

Project planning and execution
- Was the project objective clear?
- Was a detailed project plan prepared?
- Did the plan cover the full life cycle from initiating to closing?
- Did the project receive top management support throughout its life cycle?
- Was the client fully informed throughout the project?
- Was project communication effective and timely?
- Was information about the project provided in a timely manner?
- Did the project have a detailed budget?

Project deliverable
- Was the client satisfied with the final deliverable?
- How well did the final attributes match the original plan?
- What were the major variances from the original plan?

Learning from the experiences of this project
- Which project procedures need to be changed for future projects?
- How to minimize variances from the original plan in the future?
- General improvements in organizational project management?

Figure1

handling the inevitable changes to the project, and it provides a wealth of historical information for future projects. A proper project closeout will extract the usable information on all aspects of the project, for the entire project life-cycle, to be used for enhanced planning of future projects, and for more methodical reporting of the progress of future projects. Efforts committed to project planning and project closeout are clearly investments in the future of the organization. A checklist can be used to guide the project team in conducting the closeout. (Figure 6-1)

Comprehensive project planning and methodical project closeout are sometimes abbreviated in favor of short term cost savings; albeit to the long term detriment of the organization. Parenthetically, misplaced cost saving on planning and closeout of projects has an analogue in other activities of the organization. There are organizations that choose to curtail training and research in order to accommodate other financial shortfalls. Sadly, curtailing training and research is highly short-sighted and will impact the future health of the organization negatively, as would the practice of minimizing project planning and project closeout in project-oriented organizations.

Benefits of a formal close-out process to the team are that it provides a sense of accomplishment and a sense of closure, which would be invaluable for the overall morale and for the performance of future projects. Further, a formal close-out would facilitate an assurance for customer satisfaction. It could also subtly signal to the client organization that the performing organization is sophisticated, pro-active, and focused on long term enhancements. This observation could become invaluable during the evaluation of the prospective contractors for the next contract.

Termination and closeout activities include reviewing the entire project history for lessons-learned and for contractual compliance, assuring that project documents are all in order, and verifying that the client's needs and user's needs have been addressed. Then the project team will make preparations for a formal hand-over of the project deliverables and results to the client organization. There are two distinct aspects of the project closeout: technical and contractual. The technical closeout includes documenting the reasons and circumstances of termination, verifying the appropriateness of the project deliverable, and coordinating the acceptance process. Good project management practices, and proper contractual practices, require that all project activities be formally completed before the project records are closed out.

Contractual closeout includes verifying the compliance and the of the deliverable, and the performing organization, to the contract clauses. Depending on the circumstances, plans must be developed for resolving outstanding technical issues. Additionally, the project team must identify unpaid claims and back-charges, and make the painful decision of whether to forcefully pursue the payments of all charges and claims. If the client and performing organizations have to take the unfortunate route of litigation to resolve project disputes, the close-out will be extended until such time that the litigation or mediation is completed. Most client organizations and performing organizations regard litigation as a distasteful avenue of resolving contractual issues; and will take extraordinary measures to resolve the disputes in other means before resorting to full-scale litigation. The dispute resolution activities will probably include a series of negotiations for determining a reasonable value for contract price, profit, direct costs, indirect costs, and overhead. Parenthetically, it is only after all of these financial issues have been resolved that one can develop a clear picture of the profit margin of this particular contract/project.

The data collected during the close-out period can be used to provide training and mentoring for future project team members. It could also identify areas of organizational improvement in project management, proposal development, or contract management. Additionally, the proposal/contract clarity issues, and client relations issues, of this project must be reported to the proposal development team for inclusion in the proposal development best practices. Lastly, the data can be used to fine-tune the existing models that are used for predicting client satisfaction with the project, or to develop new models for that purpose.

Chapter Summary The project closeout is the formal process of characterizing the project as complete, and the contract as fulfilled. Once the entire suite of project activities have been completed and the payment for those activities have been arranged, the proposal development team would begin using this project as a prelude to other contracts from the same client, or in the same industry. In turn, the project team would begin to use the experiences of this project as a learning experience toward the performance of future projects.

References

Anonymous, *A guide to the project management body of knowledge, third edition,* Project Management Institute, Newtown Square, PA. , 2004

Bockrath, Joseph T., Contracts and the Legal Environment, McGraw Hill, New York, 1995

Cappels, Thomas M., Financially Focused Project Management, JRoss Publishers, Boca Raton, FL, 2004

Cioffi, D. Managing Project Integration. Management Concepts. Vienna, VA. 2002

Crawford, J Kent, Cabanis-Brewin J.. Optimizing Human Capital with a Strategic Project Office, Auerbach Publications, New York, 2006

DeNeufville, R; Hani, E., Bidding Models : Effects on Bidders' Risk Aversion, ASCE Journal of Construction Division, March 1977, v 103, n CO1, p 57-70

Edwards, Vernon J., Source Selection Answer Book, Management Concepts, Vienna VA, 2006

Flemming, Quentin W., Project Procurement Management, FMC Press, Tustin CA, 2003

Gates, Marvin, Bidding Model - A Monte Carlo experiment, American Society of Civil Engineers, journal of the construction division, Dec 1976, v 102, n 4, p 669-680

Gilbreath, Robert D., Managing Construction Contracts, Operational Controls for Commercial Risks, John Wiley and Sons, New York, 1992

Knutson, Joan, editor, Project Management for Business Professionals, Wiley and Sons, New York, 2001

Nutt, Howard C., Kessler, N., Levin, G., Business Development Capability Maturity Model, Shipley Associates, 2003

Rad, Parviz F., Ginger Levin, Project Portfolio Management Tools and Techniques, IIL Publishers, NYC, 2006

Rad, Parviz F., Vittal Anantatmula, Project Planning Techniques, Management Concepts, Vienna, VA, 2005

Taylor, James C., How to Cost and Price Competitive Bids, Management Concepts, Vienna, VA, 2000

Index

Accountability 94
Administrative portion 34, 55
Bid 47
Bottom-Up estimate 73
Career dimensions 101
Career track 97, 98, 99
Client focus 103
Competition 25, 50
Competition 25, 50
Compression penalty 118
Continuous improvement 31, 33, 76 123
Contract change 110, 111
Contract price 49
Contractor evaluation 63, 65
Contracts 1, 8,10,53
Cost-plus 56, 59, 60
Deliverable-Based 4
Deliverable 58, 69
Direct cost 43, 45
Earned Value concept 78, 81
Earned Value technique 79, 81
Empowerment 90, 91
Enterprise issues 21
Estimate accuracy 71
External client 84
Identify Prospects 23, 24
Internal budget 46
Internal client 84
Internally-funded 8
Legal component 34, 55
Lump-sum 56, 58, 60

Micromanage 89
Monitoring 74, 77
Optimum duration 113
Optimum cost 117
Outsourcing 3
People issues 21
Performing organization 67
Planning 35, 68
PM Sophistication 86
Prepare proposal 23, 29
Price of contract 47
Pricing strategy 49
Prioritize prospects 23, 26
Profit margin 50
Project changes 108
Project closeout, 121, 122
Project phases 13, 15
Project-Friendly 86, 87
Proposal 12, 13, 17
Proposal development 21
Proposal pipeline 32
Proposal scoring model 28
Proposal team 19, 20
Real cost 43
Reward 96
Service-Oriented, 4
Specifications 37
Technical component 34, 55
Things issues 21
Value of project 7, 8
Variable cost 43, 45
WBS 69, 70
Unit-price 62